wanda's
pie in the sky

wanda's pie in the sky

Wanda Beaver

whitecap

To the memory of my mother, a writer, who wanted me to follow in her footsteps. I did, but through the kitchen.

Edited by Elaine Jones
Proofread by Lesley Cameron
Cover and interior design by Tanya Lloyd Kyi
Author photograph by BIG RED photography—John Scully
Colour food photographs by Edward Pond
Black and white photographs by Ryan McNair
Photographs on pages 37, 44, and 59 by David Beaver
Illustrations by Francesco Galle
How-to illustrations by Wanda Beaver

Printed and bound in Canada

NATIONAL LIBRARY OF CANADA CATALOGUING IN PUBLICATION DATA
Beaver, Wanda
    Wanda's Pie in the Sky: pies, cakes, cookies, squares and more / Wanda Beaver

    Includes index.
    ISBN 1-55285-214-8

    1. Baking. 2. Pies. 3. Wanda's Pie in the Sky. I. Title
TX763.B42 2002   641.8'15   C2002-911066-1

The publisher acknowledges the support of the Canada Council and the Cultural Services Branch of the Government of British Columbia in making this publication possible. We acknowledge the financial support of the Government of Canada through the Book Publishing Industry Development Program for our publishing activities.

Important: Some of the recipes in this book call for the use of raw eggs. Pregnant women, the elderly, young children and anyone with a compromised immune system are advised against the consumption of raw eggs. You may wish to consider using pasteurized eggs. www.aeb.org/safety provides updated information on eggs and food safety.

Contents

Introduction

My love of baking began early in life. Home was in the heart of one of Canada's prime fruit-growing areas near St. Catharines along Lake Ontario. My parents were avid gardeners and our half-acre of land was a garden paradise. There were rows of pear, peach, plum and cherry trees, gooseberry, raspberry and red currant bushes and every imaginable vegetable—all interspersed with a joyous jumble of flowering bushes, perennials and rock gardens. Within this magical little kingdom were many carved mythical beasts, garden spirits and gremlins— half-hidden amid the lilac bushes, peeking from under the water lilies and lurking behind the honeysuckle-covered clapboard garage. My father's talents as a sculptor and gardener, as well as his love of the whimsical and untamed, made this an idyllic setting for the aspiring artist and baker. My brother and I spent our summer hours picking berries, eating sugar-dipped rhubarb and climbing the fruit trees to pick the bounty of fresh fruit. There always seemed to be more than could be eaten or given away. Our fruit cellar was filled with my mother's preserves, compotes and jellies. To this day I have never tasted red currant jelly as good as hers—tart, yet sweet, and just the right consistency to spread on warm buttered toast.

It was inevitable that my first foray into the realm of baking was to make a fruit pie—sour cherry, of course, still my favorite to this day. It was in the summer of 1961 that the pie gods first smiled on me; I followed a simple pastry recipe and very innocently expected it to be perfect. It was years later that I realized the art of piemaking is something that even accomplished bakers find challenging. Ah, the naiveté of a nine-year-old!

Over the decades I honed my skills, and my passion for baking continued. I always considered baking as a hobby; after all, I had much more "serious" career aspirations—I wanted to be an artist and baking was just too much fun. I was in my fourth year at the Ontario College of Art when my future beckoned.

A freshly baked peach pie opened the door to my first commercial account. I brought a pie to a friend who shared it with her roommate—a café manager. "Wow, this is delicious! Wanda, you must bake pies for our restaurant!" Little did I know what that one pie would lead to.

By the time I graduated, I was delivering my pies to several customers and others were clamoring for my wares. I put my art career on hold (temporarily, I presumed), and within a year and a half had moved my business out of my apartment into a tiny makeshift bakery. I also persuaded my husband, David, to set aside his career as an industrial designer (temporarily, of course!) and join me in my endeavor. That's not to say it wasn't a rocky beginning and it continues to have its share of trials and tribulations. But who said life is always a bowl of cherries? If it was, we would all be eating more pies!

At first it was me and my little 30-inch range, cranking out three pies at a time. Now, 15 years later, Wanda's Pie in the Sky has 20 employees, two retail locations—including a bakery-café in Toronto's popular Yorkville area—and more than 200 wholesale accounts enjoying hundreds of different products. It's not just pies anymore!

For years, friends and customers have implored me to compile a cookbook and have eagerly awaited my promise to "someday soon" fulfill this request. Writing a cookbook takes time and focus, two ingredients not readily picked up on the grocery store shelf. As much as I have tried to put it on the top of my list of priorities, I always have 10 things on the go, each one seemingly more important than the other. At a certain point, I realized that the things that give the most joy must become a priority. I love feeding people, and I take every opportunity to do so—at home, at my café, and at all the restaurants that serve my desserts. What better way to reach even more people than with a cookbook? Honestly, though, do we really need another cookbook? Absolutely! I know I'm not the only one who requires a steady diet of new and adventurous cookbooks to inspire me and send me running into the kitchen, recharged and eager to try something new. As every cook knows, there are already a zillion cookbooks out there, running the gamut from the encyclopedic to the merely decorative. I wanted to create an easy-to-use guide to desserts that was fresh, unintimidating and fun. Whether familiar classics or innovations, the recipes are flexible—leaving room to improvise, substitute and relax. I've tried to minimize the need for long chapters on tools, glossaries and basic recipes that are often required to complete an individual dish; once the basic pastries are mastered, most recipes stand on their own. Emphasis is on seasonal produce, fresh ingredients and familiar tools and terminology. And, of course, there are pictures, lots of pictures—you can't have a dessert cookbook without glossy color photos.

There is no denying that most of us adore desserts. They are associated with comfort, special occasions and pleasant memories, softening those hard edges of life and bringing a smile to everyone's face. Baking desserts should be almost as much fun as eating them—after all, what better way to inspire the baker to get back in the kitchen and produce more tantalizing treats than to make it easy and pleasurable? I hope this cookbook does just that—encouraging all aspiring bakers, as well as you old pros, to roll up your sleeves and weave your magic.

May the pie gods smile on you soon!

Wanda

Introduction to Pastry

Welcome to Wanda's Pie in the Sky introductory and remedial classes. Prepare to unravel the deep dark secrets of perfect pie crust. Fear not; if previously you have tried and failed, leaving a trail of disappointed guests and inedible desserts behind you, prepare now to not only redeem yourself in the eyes of your family and friends, but to knock their socks off with your unbelievable pies. I promise you: it is not as difficult as it seems.

PIE CRUST 101

The first thing I ask the students in any of my pastry classes is how many of them have made pies before. Of the half or so who respond in the affirmative, I ask how many have made pies that were actually eaten. Between the chuckles and the moans I gather that the problem is invariably in the crust. It is either too dry to roll out (resulting in no pie at all—just filling) or so gooey and soft that it tears and sticks when rolled (resulting in a messy pie). Quite often, if it is easy to roll out, it tastes and feels like cardboard when baked.

When I made my first pie, it must have been by pure luck that it turned out well enough for me to do it a second, third and fourth time, because I sure enough did. Although luck is always welcome, the art of making pie crusts (and it certainly is an art) is something that combines not just understanding of ingredients and technique, but, most importantly, experience. In other words—practice, practice, practice! It is valuable to know, for example, why your crust came out so impossibly dry.

Is it a result of undermixing the flour and fat before adding the water, or perhaps not enough water, or maybe not enough fat.... Or is it something else altogether? (You see, at this point it seems very complicated, doesn't it?) But after actually doing it a few times (with some instructions as you go), all these problems will be merely academic and, as always, experience will turn out to be the best teacher.

Before you begin, do your homework! You say you hated physics and chemistry in high school? Maybe if you got to eat your projects at the end of each class, it would have been more enjoyable. Baking is definitely physics and chemistry, and a few basic rules can be very helpful.

First of all, let's talk about ingredients. It is a good place to start because there are very few ingredients in pastry.

FLOUR: There are three types of flour: hard wheat flour, all-purpose flour and soft wheat flour. When using U.S. cookbooks, be aware that they differentiate between cake flour and pastry flour as two distinct types. What we need to know is what makes all these flours different from each other.

Bread flour is for making—guess what? That's right—bread. And bread requires flour with a high gluten content, which is hard wheat flour. Gluten is a protein in wheat. When water is added to flour and the mixture is kneaded, the gluten causes it to become very elastic and stretchy. In bread this is desirable—the yeast needs that elasticity to allow the dough to rise. However, in pastry active gluten will create a tough crust. But this doesn't mean that we need a flour with a very low gluten content, such as cake and pastry flour. In fact, low-gluten flour would make a dough so delicate it might fall apart before we could get it into the pie plate, and when baked it would be far too tender to hold up to a filling. That leaves us with all-purpose flour, a blend of both high-gluten and low-gluten flour. Canadian all-purpose flour has a slightly lower gluten content than American all-purpose flour, and I find it to be ideal for making pastry. Canadian wheat produces superb flour and, honestly, I do not find much difference among the various brands. Just open the bag and scoop—when making pies, sifting isn't even necessary. The only thing left to decide is whether it will be bleached or unbleached. Personally, I prefer to use unbleached flour whenever possible—there is virtually no difference in the final color and the advantage is one less chemical in my food.

Enough about flour, let's move onto ingredient number two: fat.

FAT: Not a four-letter word, as some would have you believe, but an essential ingredient for making pastry. It is what gives the crust flavor and makes it flaky, tender and crisp. Not all fats are created equal; they differ in three important ways—flavor, melting temperature and fat content, all things that must be taken into consideration when making pastry.

When it comes to flavor, butter is best—much maligned and picked on, but secretly adored by all (don't deny it, no one

believes you anymore!). The flavor of butter and the crispness and golden color it creates in a pie makes it the best choice by far for pastry. That's not to say other fats have nothing to offer, and combining different fats can often yield the best results.

What vegetable shortening lacks in richness of flavor, it makes up for in the flakiness it produces. This is because it has a much higher melting temperature than butter. When the unbaked crust made with shortening goes in the oven, the flour and water components in the dough begin to set before the shortening melts, thus producing flaky layers. Butter melts almost immediately when placed in the oven, creating a more homogeneous texture. To illustrate the high melting point of shortening, just try washing shortening off your hands under even the hottest water—impossible without soap, whereas butter melts as soon as you touch it.

The third difference between butter and shortening is fat content. Shortening is 100% fat, compared to 80–85% for butter (the rest is liquid; this requires some adjustments when adding liquid in the recipe—more on that later).

Unfortunately, now we must talk about...lard. Sorry! I know your grandmother would argue, but I would never combine pig fat and strawberries, and it's my book, so there!

LIQUID: The third important ingredient in pastry is liquid. Liquid, in the form of water and possibly eggs and cream, activates the gluten in the flour, giving strength and structure to the pastry. Without any liquid, the pastry would not hold together and would be impossible to roll out. Since butter contains some water, pastry recipes containing butter usually include less additional liquid than the ones high in shortening, which is (as mentioned earlier) pure fat.

You may find many recipes call for additional ingredients, such as vinegar, in pie pastry. The acid in vinegar tends to soften the gluten in the pastry, making it less elastic, easier to roll and also less liable to shrink when baked. I have found, however, that if the dough is allowed to rest for 20 to 30 minutes before rolling and is chilled thoroughly before baking, this relaxes the gluten sufficiently. I prefer not to use vinegar in my pastry, as I am not particularly fond of the taste it produces.

SALT: If omitted, no one will notice. If included, however, it adds a little magic, enhancing the sweetness and rounding out the flavors wonderfully.

Now that we've talked about ingredients, let's move on to tools and technique. Raw materials of the right kind and quality are crucial, but just as the finest paints and a quality canvas are not enough to paint a masterpiece, the best ingredients when baking can produce mediocre or even disastrous results without the proper technique. Once you've had lots of practice, you'll be able to make a pie crust in no time flat. However, in the beginning, give yourself lots of time and, most importantly, relax. Most mistakes are caused by rushing and almost every problem can be repaired or even averted if caught in time.

TROUBLESHOOTING

QUESTION NUMBER 1

"I like to cook by how things feel. I never measure my ingredients and my stuff always comes out great—except for my pies. Why?"
When making pasta, a bit more garlic and a little olive oil will not make much difference; when making pastry, even a bit too much butter or a few tablespoons less water can have serious consequences. Baking is not like cooking. Even slight variations in measurements can drastically change the end result. Don't guess. Measure carefully, and use wet measuring cups for all liquids and dry measuring cups for all dry ingredients. Be sure to level dry ingredients with a knife or spatula, and pour liquids into measuring cups that are sitting on the counter rather than in your hand. A little extra care at this point can make all the difference.

QUESTION NUMBER 2

"Can I use a food processor to make pie pastry?"
The answer to this question is "yes" and "no." Even though a food processor is easy and fast to use and works well for pastry—especially when making an all-butter crust—I always prefer the control you have when cutting by hand using a traditional pastry cutter. The design of this type of cutter has not changed since your grandmother's days. (I have some antique cutters that are virtually identical to ones made today.) When choosing a pastry cutter look for one with rigid, generously spaced wires, a round wooden handle, and a bolt on the end that can be tightened when it becomes loose (and it will). Avoid the ones with flat plastic handles, flimsy prongs and

cheesy little bolts that always loosen and can't be tightened—they are frustrating and ridiculous. Although not as bad, the solid metal cutter with the flat metal sides is also not ideal; the goal of cutting pastry is to cut, not squish, and these flat sides tend to cream the fat instead of cutting it, especially when making a larger batch of pastry.

QUESTION NUMBER 3

"Am I overmixing? My dough is always so dry and falls apart when I roll it!"

In the hundreds of classes I have taught, this is one of the most frequently asked questions. And guess what—the answer is exactly the opposite. Usually most people have such a fear of overmixing the pastry that they drastically undermix, adding the water too soon and creating an uneven mix of flour, water and fat that is very difficult to roll out. In fact, adding water when the fat particles are large and the flour is still very much separate causes the water to combine with the flour, activating the gluten much more and causing a tougher crust. By undermixing, not only will the dough be difficult to roll out, it may actually turn out tougher. Certainly it is possible to overmix, but in the beginning it is best to mix a little more thoroughly before adding the water because the pastry will be a little easier to roll. As you become more practiced, add the water a bit sooner, the result will be slightly drier when rolling, but also flakier when baked.

QUESTION NUMBER 4
"So how do I tell when it's been mixed enough before I add my water?"
Cut until the mixture resembles coarse meal and is just beginning to clump together. Rather than adding a bit of the water at a time and mixing after each addition, I find sprinkling all of it evenly over the surface works best. If the mixture is perfectly cut, the water will virtually disappear almost immediately. If it is undermixed it will sit on top for a while before sinking in. If it is overmixed, the water will pool on the bottom of the bowl. Wait for about 30 seconds, cut the water into the dough using about 12 to 15 strokes and then gather the pastry into a ball. That's it. Rather than kneading it too much with your hands,

whack it a few times on the rolling surface to compress it. Don't worry if there are a few wet streaks or dry areas, they will even out when the dough rests. Press into a disk, wrap in plastic, and chill for at least 20 to 30 minutes.

QUESTION NUMBER 5

"Why can't I use the pastry right away? Is it really necessary to chill it?"

Have you ever made a crust that looked great when it went in the oven and then was considerably smaller when it came out? This shrinkage will definitely occur if the dough is not allowed to rest in the refrigerator. First of all, the chilling keeps the layers of fat, flour and water intact and makes the dough firmer. Secondly, the stretchy gluten—which is activated when the water is added—will relax and lose most of its elasticity. If the dough is popped in the oven right away, the gluten will spring back, causing the crust to shrink. When baking a crust without a filling, chill the rolled-out crust thoroughly before baking. This will help the crust keep its shape and prevent puffing. (See Question number 11, page 27, for more on this.) For filled pies, a second chilling after the pie crust is rolled and filled, before it is baked, is recommended to produce the maximum flakiness.

QUESTION NUMBER 6

"My dough always sticks to the counter when I roll it and I get so frustrated I just ball it up and re-roll it. What am I doing wrong?"

Don't be afraid to use flour liberally to dust your rolling area. If the pastry is sufficiently cool and firm, it will not absorb too much flour, but insufficient flour will cause sticking. Secondly, keep that circle of pastry moving! Rotate it a bit every few rolls, keep the top dusted with flour and flip it occasionally before it gets too big. Repair any cracks along the outside edges by wetting them lightly, overlapping and pressing firmly. Dust lightly with flour and keep rolling. Remember, any tears and holes can be repaired with minimum loss of flakiness—just wet and patch. Better to patch than to reroll the dough. Rerolling definitely toughens pastry.

QUESTION NUMBER 7
"How do you get the dough into the pie plate without tearing it?"
First of all, relax. Any tear can be repaired once the pastry is in the plate. The easiest way to transfer the rolled circle into the pie plate is to wrap it around the rolling pin, center it over the plate and then unroll it. With a small pie, just lifting it with your hands underneath for support works well.

Folding it in half, transferring it manually onto the plate and then unfolding it is also not too difficult, especially with a small pie. If the dough breaks on the fold, just wet, overlap and press firmly. If the circle of dough is too small to allow overlapping, patch with additional dough and water. Just avoid stretching the dough in all cases. Once in the plate, gently push the pastry into the bottom corners of the plate, making sure there are no gaps.

QUESTION NUMBER 8
"When I trim the dough and put the top crust on, there appears to be enough pastry, but when the pie bakes the edges always shrink, the filling overflows, the pie ends up looking messy and I can't get the slices out of the plate! Help!"
Pie crust is delicious, so why not be generous with it? The less you cut off, the more there is to eat. As well, an ample edge means more filling can be put in the pie before it overflows. The result is more crust, more filling and, therefore, more pie for everybody! When you roll out the bottom crust, make sure it is a good 1½ inches (3.8 cm) bigger than the actual pie plate. This will give you a ¾-inch (1.8-cm) overhang once the crust is in the plate. Fold this overhang under itself, making sure that the edge is still slightly larger than the plate below. This will give you something to hold on to when you flute the edges. For

a double crust pie, wet the edge slightly and place the top crust or lattice strips just short of the edges. Press firmly and then flute decoratively.

QUESTION NUMBER 9

"I can't make a pie edge—mine always looks so uneven and droopy. What is the secret?"

The answer to this question is a little trickier than to the others. To make a nice fluted edge takes practice, nimble fingers, and more practice. However, there are a few pointers to make the task easier. First, make sure the crust is evenly turned under all the way around, with an ample edge. It shouldn't be too big, though, or it will droop in the oven. But don't make it too small either, or you'll have nothing to grab on to! (I know, I know, it's getting way too complicated! But fear not, it can be done!) Secondly, pre-mark the spots where you want to flute by folding the dough between the index fingers and pushing lightly out with the thumbs, about a finger's width apart. Mark around the crust in this way and then do a classic flute by making a

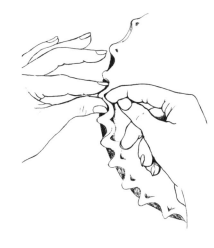

v-shape with the left-hand thumb and index finger and pushing out with the right index finger. Thirdly, as you look down onto the edge of the pie, make sure that the pie plate is still barely visible. This will ensure an edge that neither droops nor shrinks when baked. Last but not least, chill the assembled pie before baking for at least 30 minutes to help the crust hold its shape when baking and to keep it flaky.

QUESTION NUMBER 10

"My pies sometimes have a soft, underbaked crust on the bottom. If I bake them longer, until the bottom is golden, the edges and the filling get overdone. What can I do?"

First of all, check your oven temperature. An oven that is too hot will definitely burn the edges long before the filling is fully cooked.

The second possible solution to underbaked bottom crusts is to make larger pies. The logic behind this is simple: the larger

the pie, the longer it takes to bake and the more time the bottom crust has to brown. This is especially true of custard pies like pumpkin. Since eggs cook relatively quickly, a shallow custard pie filling sets well before the crust has time to bake. The bigger the pie, the longer it needs to bake and the more chance there is for the bottom to brown.

Thirdly, try using glass plates. Glass browns better than tin or aluminum and as a bonus, you can actually see the color of the pastry through the glass.

Finally, if you're using a pan under the pie to catch any drips, preheat the pan before baking to help transfer heat quickly to the bottom crust, thus ensuring it will brown more quickly.

QUESTION NUMBER 11

"How can I bake an unfilled pie crust without it puffing up or shrinking?"

This is called "blind baking" and can be a real challenge. For certain pies, such as lemon meringue, coconut cream or chocolate mousse, the filling is prepared separately from the pastry, which is prebaked. Left to its own devices and baked without something to weigh it down, the crust can puff up like a balloon, droop, shrink or become misshapen.

The customary way to prepare crusts for blind baking is to line the unbaked pie shell with foil or parchment paper, and then fill it with either beans or metal pie weights before baking. The advantages of using foil over parchment paper are two-fold. Metal conducts heat faster and more efficiently than paper, making for a more golden crust. And foil is more flexible than parchment paper and can be molded to the shape of the crust, ensuring an even surface with no ballooning or droopy edges after baking.

As for the question of beans versus pie weights, although beans will work in a pinch, I strongly advise investing in some metal pie weights. They are readily available in most baking supply stores and last forever (although I have used pennies in a pinch). Just as foil conducts heat better than parchment paper, metal weights also heat quicker and more efficiently than beans, ensuring the bottom of the crust browns as quickly as the exposed edges. Metal weights are heavier than beans, firmly holding down the bottom, and especially the sides, of the pie crust. This prevents slipping and shrinking, thereby creating a uniform crust. I have to confess that at the bakery we do not use any of these methods. We make so many blind crusts at one time that it became necessary to come up with a less time-consuming method for holding down the pastry. If you can live with a pie crust that is about 99% as flaky, golden and tender as one baked using traditional pie weights and foil, then feel free to try this quick and lazy method.

Simply place a metal or foil pie plate of the same size over the unbaked pie crust, making sure it fits snugly and is not actually bigger (slightly smaller is fine) than the pie crust. If the top plate is light, weigh it down with a heavier pan or bowl (ovenproof glass bowls are perfect for this). Bake exactly as when using tin foil and pie weights, which is as follows.

Once you have rolled the rested, chilled pastry, fitted it into the plate and fluted it, before you line it with foil and weights and bake it, chill it thoroughly for at least 30 to 45 minutes. Why so long? When the chilled pastry hits the hot oven, the flour sets quicker than the cold fat, producing wonderfully flaky layers and virtually no shrinking or drooping. It is crucial to remove the weights and lining part-way through the baking, otherwise the crust will be compressed and lacking in flakiness. Baking time varies, but I have found with a 400°F (200°C) oven (hot enough to bake the pastry quickly but not so hot it browns the edges too much), 15 to 20 minutes is long enough to set the pastry, after which time the weights can be removed and the crust can continue to bake another 10 minutes or so, until golden. That's it, now you know all about blind crusts, so proceed immediately to the lemon meringue pie recipe and get busy!

QUESTION NUMBER 12
"What about crusts with chocolate or nuts—can they be made the same way?"
This technique for blind crusts applies to sweet crusts as well, either rolled or pressed. Baking time may decrease due to the

browning effect of the sugar. Some crusts, because they contain larger quantities of nuts, cocoa or chocolate, thus making them more stable, can actually be baked blind without any weights.

After much experimentation, I have found that I prefer sweet dough without the addition of eggs—whites in particular. Although adding eggs makes for a sturdier texture, the result is slightly tougher, there is a tendency for more puffing and, frankly, the taste is, well . . . eggy.

Pricking the crust before baking is optional. I have found it has little effect on the puffing of the pastry when baking and I usually skip that step. However, chilling is just as important in sweet crusts as in the basic pastry to ensure good definition and minimize shrinking, which is more likely due to the vertical sides of the flan pan usually used when baking sweet crusts.

Parchment Paper

I'm a great believer in the use of parchment paper whenever possible. It saves on clean-up, prevents sticking and scorching, and keeps your pans looking new and is reusable. What's not to like? Certainly, if you are in the habit of greasing your pans or if you do not have parchment paper in your cupboard—by all means, grease away. However, I strongly suggest you give parchment paper a try. It is readily available in all baking supply stores.

Single Crust Pastry

Makes pastry for one 10-inch (25-cm) single crust pie

1 ½ cups (360 mL) all-purpose
   flour

¼ tsp. (1.2 mL) salt

⅓ cup (80 mL) cold butter,
   cut into ½-inch (1.2-cm)
   pieces

⅓ cup (80 mL) shortening,
   cut into ½-inch (1.2-cm)
   pieces and frozen for
   15 minutes

¼ cup (60 mL) cold water

This is an all-purpose pastry—perfect for pies, tarts and turnovers, as well as for savory items such as quiche or meat pies.

Make sure all the ingredients are as cold as possible. Using a food processor or a pastry cutter and a large bowl, combine the flour, salt, butter and shortening. Process or cut in until the mixture resembles coarse meal and begins to clump together. Sprinkle with the water, let rest for 30 seconds and then either process very briefly or cut with about 15 strokes of the pastry cutter, just until the dough begins to stick together and come away from the sides of the bowl. Turn onto a lightly floured work surface and press together to form a disk. Wrap in plastic and chill for at least 20 minutes.

Allow the dough to warm slightly at room temperature if it is too hard to roll. On a lightly floured board, roll the disk to a thickness of ⅛ inch (.3 cm). Cut a circle about 1 ½ inches (3.8 cm) larger than the pie plate. Transfer the pastry to the plate by folding it in half or by rolling it onto the rolling pin. Turn the pastry under, leaving an edge that hangs about ½ inch (1.2 cm) over the plate. Flute the edges. Use as directed in recipe.

Double Crust Pastry

Makes pastry for one 10-inch (25-cm) double crust pie

2¼ cups (535 mL) all-purpose flour

¼ tsp. (1.2 mL) salt

½ cup (120 mL) cold butter, cut into ½-inch (1.2-cm) pieces

½ cup (120 mL) shortening, cut into ½-inch (1.2-cm) pieces and frozen for 15 minutes

⅓ cup (80 mL) cold water

Make sure all the ingredients are as cold as possible. Using a food processor or a pastry cutter and a large bowl, combine the flour, salt, butter and shortening. Process or cut in until the mixture resembles coarse meal and begins to clump together. Sprinkle with the water, let rest for 30 seconds and then either process very briefly or cut with about 15 strokes of the pastry cutter, just until the dough begins to stick together and come away from the sides of the bowl. Turn onto a lightly floured work surface and press together to form a short cylinder. Divide into ⅔ and ⅓ and press into disks. Wrap in plastic and chill for at least 20 minutes.

Allow the dough to warm slightly at room temperature if it is too hard to roll. On a lightly floured board, roll the larger disk to a thickness of ⅛ inch (.3 cm). Cut a circle about 1½ inches (3.8 cm) larger than the pie plate and transfer the pastry to the plate by folding it in half or by rolling it onto the rolling pin. Turn the pastry under, leaving an edge that hangs about ½ inch (1.2 cm) over the plate. Roll the second disk as directed by the recipe.

Basic Sweet Pastry

Makes pastry for one 10-inch (25-cm) flan, two 8-inch (20-cm) tarts or one dozen 3-inch (7.5-cm) tarts

1 cup (240 mL) cold butter, cut into ½-inch (1.2-cm) pieces

2¼ cups (535 mL) all-purpose flour

⅓ cup (80 mL) cornstarch

¼ tsp. (1.2 mL) salt

⅓ cup (80 mL) granulated sugar

⅓ cup (80 mL) cold water

This is an extremely tender, melt-in-your mouth crust, due to the addition of cornstarch, which gives it the texture of a shortbread cookie. Chill it thoroughly before rolling it out, but allow it to soften slightly to make it easier to work with. It tears easily but it can be patched simply by pressing it firmly. To make your life even easier, just press it into the pan and trim the edges, instead of rolling it.

Preheat the oven to 375°F (190°C).

Using a food processor or pastry blender, combine the butter, flour, cornstarch, salt and sugar and cut in until the mixture is crumbly and beginning to clump. Add the water and combine until it just comes together. Do not overprocess. Press into a 10 x 1¼-inch (25 x 3-cm) flan pan with a removable bottom. Chill for 30 minutes. Use as directed in recipe.

Basic Chocolate Pastry

Makes pastry for one 10-inch (25-cm) flan, two 8-inch (20-cm) tarts or one dozen 3-inch (7.5-cm) tarts

1 cup (240 ml) cold butter, cut into ½-inch (1.2-cm) pieces

1⅓ cups (320 mL) all-purpose flour

⅓ cup (80 mL) pastry flour

⅔ cup (160 mL) cocoa

¾ cup (180 mL) icing sugar

¼ tsp.(1.2 mL) salt

¼ cup (60 mL) water

A crispy bittersweet cookie of a crust, this pastry is pressed into the pan rather than rolled. I find it shrinks very little and holds its shape wonderfully. Substitute this crust in any recipe for cream, custard or mousse pie, for that extra chocolate kick. For a sweeter version, decrease the cocoa from ⅔ cup (160 mL) to ⅓ cup (80 mL) and increase the icing sugar from ¾ cup (180 mL) to 1¼ cups (300 mL).

Preheat the oven to 375°F (190°C)

Using a food processor or pastry blender combine the butter, flour, pastry flour, cocoa, icing sugar and salt and cut in until crumbly and beginning to clump. Add the water and combine until the mixture just comes together. Do not overprocess. Press into a 10 x 1¼-inch (25 x 3-cm) flan pan with a removable bottom. Chill for 30 minutes. Line with foil and pie weights or beans. Bake for 15 minutes until firm. Remove the foil and continue baking for 10 minutes, or as directed in the recipe.

Fruit Pies and Desserts

To me, the word "pie" conjures up a vision of a deep, lattice-topped fruit pie, the pastry golden and fragrant, the filling hot and bubbly from the oven. A pie made of fruit is the quintessential pie, nature's bounty only slightly tamed, wholesome yet delightfully sensual—the perfect dessert. The ideal fruit pie is a contradiction of components: a juicy, slightly runny filling in a crisp, flaky crust. These contrasting elements are what gives a fruit pie its unique appeal, but creating that perfect balance can be a challenge. Having baked thousands of pies in my day and having taught numerous pie-baking classes, I can confidently say that, with the mastery of a few basic principles and a relaxed attitude, everyone can bake the perfect pie.

I've also included a number of desserts that can't make up their minds if they are fruit pies or cakes. Whether nestled in a tender cake batter or covered with flaky pastry, there is one ingredient all the desserts in this chapter have in common: sweet, juicy fruit, and lots of it!

Ontario Sour Cherry Pie

Makes one 10-inch (25-cm) pie (serves 8)

1 recipe Double Crust Pastry
  (page 32)
6½ cups (1.6 L) pitted sour
  cherries, fresh or frozen
1 cup (240 mL) granulated
  sugar (more or less,
  depending on the tartness
  of the cherries)
3 Tbsp. (45 mL) cornstarch
½ tsp. (2.5 mL) almond
  extract
1 egg beaten with 1 Tbsp.
  (15 mL) cold water
1 Tbsp. (15 mL) granulated
  sugar

I absolutely adore cherries! This is the first pie I ever baked. I was just nine years old and yes, it is still my favorite. For me, sour cherries are the ideal fruit for a pie—juicy, intensely flavored and gorgeous to look at. I guarantee those nasty memories of gloppy, canned cherry pie filling will be dispelled with one tart-sweet bite of a freshly baked sour cherry pie.

Prepare the pastry as directed, setting aside the smaller disk. Preheat the oven to 400°F (200°C).

In a large bowl mix together the cherries, 1 cup (240 mL) sugar, cornstarch and almond extract. Turn into the prepared crust, leaving room at the edges for sealing and crimping the pastry.

On a lightly floured board, roll out the remaining disk of dough ⅛ inch (.3 cm) thick. Cut into fourteen ¾-inch (1.8-cm) strips using a knife or decorative crimper. Cut three 1-inch (2.5-cm) cherries, three 2 x ⅛-inch (5 x .3-cm) cherry stems and two 2-inch (5-cm) leaves out of the remaining pastry. Weave a lattice, beginning at the center of the pie. Trim the strips, seal and flute the edges. Place the decorative pastry cutouts to resemble 3 cherries joined into 2 leaves. Brush with the egg wash and sprinkle with the remaining 1 Tbsp. (15 mL) sugar.

If time allows, chill for 30 minutes. Bake for 10 minutes and then reduce the temperature to 350°F (175°C). Bake for 50 to 60 minutes, until the crust is golden and the filling is bubbling in the center. Serve slightly warm or at room temperature. Store lightly covered at room temperature for up to 2 days.

Sour Cherries

The availability of sour cherries varies, depending where you live. Our American cousins are fortunate to have cherries readily available in the frozen fruit section of their grocery stores, but in Canada it takes a bit more effort to find them. Buy them in pails from the farmer in mid-July, portion them into freezer bags, and have enough for the entire winter. I live in Toronto near a Polish area and during July baskets of sour cherries abound—Polish people being great lovers of this fruit. I am absolutely thrilled that I can get my fill and I always make the most of the season.

Traditional Covered Apple Pie

Makes one 10-inch (23-cm) pie (serves 8)

1 recipe Double Crust Pastry
(page 32)

7 cups (1.75 L) tart apples,
peeled and cut into ¼-inch
(.6-cm) slices

½ cup (120 mL) granulated
sugar

2 Tbsp. (30 mL) cornstarch

2 tsp. (10 mL) lemon juice

1 tsp. (5 mL) ground cinnamon

½ tsp. (2.5 mL) ground
nutmeg

2 Tbsp. (30 mL) butter

1 egg beaten with 1 Tbsp.
(15 mL) cold water

1 Tbsp. (15 mL) granulated
sugar

Apples are the most charming, delicious and versatile of fruits. They are equally at home in a rustic crumble or a delicate tarte tatin. Ideally, apples best suited for pies are tart, firm and juicy. Spies, Cortlands, Ida Reds and Matsus are all great choices, but don't hesitate to use two or more varieties together in a pie. A crispy Spy mixed with a fragrant Red Delicious and a juicy Macintosh will yield a superb balance of textures and flavors.

Prepare the pastry as directed, setting aside the smaller disk. Preheat the oven to 400°F (200°C).

In a large bowl mix together the apples, ½ cup (120 mL) sugar, cornstarch, lemon juice, cinnamon and nutmeg. Turn into the prepared crust, leaving room at the edges for sealing and crimping the top crust. Dot with the butter. On a floured board roll out the remaining disk of dough into a circle ⅛ inch (.3 cm) thick. Cut a circle the size of the pie plate. Cut vents in the dough to allow the steam to escape. Wet the edges of the pie crust, and place the pastry circle over the fruit. Seal and flute the edges. Brush with the egg wash and sprinkle with the 1 Tbsp. (15 mL) sugar. If time allows, refrigerate for 30 minutes.

Bake for 10 minutes and then reduce the oven temperature to 350°F (175°C). Bake for 50 to 60 minutes, or until the pastry is golden and the filling is bubbly. Serve warm or at room temperature. Store lightly covered at room temperature for up to 2 days.

VARIATIONS

APPLE CRUMBLE: Prepare as above but reduce the sugar to ¼ cup (60 mL) and use only the bottom crust. Flute the edges of the crust. Place ½ cup (120 mL) cold butter, cut into ½-inch (1.2-cm) pieces, ½ cup (120 mL) brown sugar, ½ cup (120 mL) sugar and 1 cup (240 mL) all-purpose flour in the food processor and mix until it begins to clump. Cover the filling with the crumble mixture and bake as above.

DUTCH APPLE PIE: Prepare as for Apple Crumble and add 1 cup (240 mL) sour cream mixed with 1 egg to the fruit. Cover with the crumble mixture.

SWISS APPLE PIE: Prepare filling as for Traditional Covered Apple Pie but add 1 cup (240 mL) milk mixed with 1 egg, 1 tsp. (5 mL) vanilla extract and 1 tsp. (5 mL) lemon zest to the fruit.

Apple Raspberry Pie

Makes one 10-inch (25-cm) pie (serves 8)

1 recipe Double Crust Pastry
  (page 32)
4½ cups (1.1 L) apples,
  peeled and cut into ¼-inch
  (.6-cm) slices
2 cups (475 mL) raspberries,
  fresh or frozen
⅔ cup (160 mL) granulated
  sugar
3 Tbsp. (45 mL) cornstarch
½ tsp. (2.5 mL) almond
  extract
1 egg beaten with 1 Tbsp.
  (15 mL) cold water
1 Tbsp. (15 mL) granulated
  sugar
1 cup (240 mL) whipping
  cream

A marriage made in pie heaven, this pie is a perfect balance of texture, flavor and color and is definitely best served warm. The gorgeous rosy filling contrasts wonderfully with the crisp flaky crust and the tartness of the fruit is mellowed by the rich cream. The diagonal lattice is an interesting variation, but don't worry if it is too much of a challenge, just do a regular lattice.

Prepare the pastry as directed, setting aside the smaller disk. Preheat the oven to 400°F (200°C).

In a large bowl mix together the apples, raspberries, ⅔ cup (160 mL) sugar, cornstarch and almond extract. Turn into the prepared crust, leaving room at the edges for sealing and crimping the top pastry.

On a lightly floured board, roll out the remaining disk of dough into a circle ⅛ inch (.3 cm) thick. Cut it into ten ¾-inch (1.8-cm) strips using a knife or decorative crimper. Wet the edges of the crust and weave a lattice on the diagonal. To do this, begin with one piece in the center of the pie. Place the second piece across it diagonally at a 45-degree angle. Continue as for a regular lattice, except at a 45-degree angle instead of a 90-degree angle. It takes a little practice. Seal and flute the edges. Brush with the egg wash and sprinkle with the 1 Tbsp. (15 mL) sugar. Chill the pie for 30 minutes before baking, if possible.

Bake for 10 minutes and then reduce the temperature to 350°F (175°C). Bake for 50 to 60 minutes, until the crust is golden and the filling is bubbling in the center. Remove from the oven and pour the whipping cream through the openings in the lattice crust. It is not necessary to pour in more than 4 spots, as the cream will spread throughout the pie. Best served warm. Store in the refrigerator for up to 3 days. Bring to room temperature before serving.

Apple Crimson Berry Pie

Makes one 10-inch (25-cm) pie, (serves 8)

1 recipe Double Crust Pastry
(page 32)

4 cups (950 mL) peeled and
cored apples cut into
¼-inch (.6-cm) slices

¾ cup (180 mL) wild blue-
berries, fresh or frozen

1 cup (240 mL) cranberries,
fresh or frozen

¾ cup (180 mL) sour cherries,
fresh or frozen

⅔ cup (160 mL) granulated
sugar

3 Tbsp. (45 mL) cornstarch

1 Tbsp. (15 mL) lemon juice

½ tsp. (2.5 mL) ground
cinnamon

1 tsp. (5 mL) orange zest

1 egg beaten with 1 Tbsp.
(15 mL) cold water

1 Tbsp. (15 mL) butter,
softened

2 Tbsp. (30 mL) brown sugar

2 Tbsp. (30 mL) all-purpose
flour

2 Tbsp. (30 mL) quick-cook
rolled oats (not regular
or instant)

2 Tbsp. (30 mL) coarsely
chopped walnuts

Combining blueberries, cranberries and cherries with the apples gives this gorgeous pie a rich, royal red color. The mixture of berries and apples makes it very juicy and gives it a great texture. The cinnamon and orange zest add intense flavor notes and the walnut crumble, a wonderful crunch.

Prepare the pastry as directed, setting aside the smaller disk. Preheat the oven to 400°F (200°C).

In a large bowl mix together the apples, blueberries, cran-berries, cherries, granulated sugar, cornstarch, lemon juice, cinnamon and orange zest. Turn into the prepared crust, leav-ing room at the edges for sealing and crimping the top crust.

On a lightly floured board roll out the remaining disk of dough into a circle ⅛ inch (.3 cm) thick. Cut into six ½-inch (1.2-cm) strips using a knife or decorative crimper. Weave a lattice, beginning at the center of the pie. Trim the strips, seal and flute the edges. Brush with the egg wash.

In a small bowl, combine the butter, brown sugar, flour and rolled oats. Using your fingertips, crumble it until it resembles coarse meal. Mix in the walnuts and sprinkle the mixture over the pie.

If time allows, chill for 30 minutes. Bake for 10 minutes, reduce the oven temperature to 350°F (175°C) and bake for 50 to 60 minutes, or until it's bubbly in the center. Serve warm or at room temperature. Store lightly covered at room tempera-ture for up to 2 days.

Apple Cherry Crumble Pie

Makes one 10-inch (25-cm) pie (serves 8)

1 recipe Single Crust Pastry (page 31)

⅓ cup (80 mL) cold butter, cut into ½-inch (1.2-cm) pieces

⅓ cup (80 mL) brown sugar

⅓ cup (80 mL) all-purpose flour

⅔ cup (160 mL) quick-cook rolled oats (not regular or instant)

3½ cups (840 mL) apples, peeled and cut into ¼-inch (.6-cm) slices

3 cups (720 mL) pitted sour cherries

¼ cup (60 mL) granulated sugar

1 Tbsp. (15 mL) cornstarch

1 tsp. (5 mL) ground cinnamon

½ tsp. (2.5 mL) almond extract

¼ cup (60 mL) sliced almonds

You will love this pie! The combination of apples, cherries, cinnamon, almonds and oatmeal crumble produces a truly outstanding dessert. Delightfully tangy, with the sweet surprise of crumbly brown sugar and toasted almonds.

Prepare the pastry as directed. Preheat the oven to 400°F (200°C).

Using a food processor or pastry blender, cut the butter into the brown sugar and flour. Process until the mixture just begins to clump. Add the oats and process for a few seconds, just to combine.

In a large bowl mix together the apples, cherries, granulated sugar, cornstarch, cinnamon and almond extract. Turn into the prepared crust. Pile the crumble mixture loosely on top of the pie. Do not press it down. Sprinkle with the almonds.

If time allows, refrigerate for 30 minutes. Bake for 10 minutes and then reduce the oven temperature to 350°F (175°C). Bake for 50 to 60 minutes, or until the pastry is golden and the filling is bubbly. Serve warm or at room temperature. Store lightly covered at room temperature for up to 2 days.

Strawberry Rhubarb Pie

Makes one 10-inch (25-cm) pie (serves 8)

1 recipe Double Crust Pastry
(page 32)

4½ cups (1.1 L) rhubarb fresh
or frozen, cut into ½-inch
(1.2-cm) pieces

2 cups (475 mL) strawberries,
fresh or frozen

¾ to 1 cup (180 to 240 mL)
granulated sugar (depend-
ing on the tartness of the
rhubarb)

3 Tbsp. (45 mL) cornstarch

1 egg beaten with 1 Tbsp.
(15 mL) cold water

1 Tbsp. (15 mL) granulated
sugar

The fans of this fruit pie are legion! Make it to celebrate the first welcome crops of spring. The tart, lively taste of crisp rhubarb is a perfect match for the sweet juiciness of ripe strawberries.

Prepare the pastry as directed, setting aside the smaller disk. Preheat the oven to 400°F (200°C).

Cut the strawberries into smaller pieces if they are very large. In a large bowl mix together the strawberries, rhubarb, ¾ to 1 cup (180 to 240 mL) sugar and cornstarch. Turn into the prepared crust, leaving room at the edges for sealing and crimp-ing the pastry. On a lightly floured board roll out the remaining disk of dough into a circle ⅛ inch (.3 cm) thick. Cut it into ten ¾-inch (1.8-cm) strips, using a knife or decorative crimper. Weave a lattice, beginning at the center of the pie. Trim the strips, seal and flute the edges. Brush with egg wash and sprinkle with the 1 Tbsp. (15 mL) sugar.

If time allows, chill for 30 minutes. Bake for 10 minutes, reduce the temperature to 350°F (175°C), and bake for 50 to 60 minutes, until the crust is golden and the filling is bubbling in the center. Serve slightly warm or at room temperature. Store lightly covered at room temperature for up to 2 days.

Freezing Strawberries and Rhubarb

Both strawberries and rhubarb freeze beautifully with very little preparation and are available inexpensively in the spring and early summer. Freeze the strawberries whole and the rhubarb in 1-inch (2.5-cm) pieces (smaller for very thick stalks.) Place them in single layers on a baking sheet and transfer to freezer bags when frozen solid. Measure frozen fruit as for fresh when preparing the pie, allowing the fruit to thaw slightly before bak-ing. Increase your baking time by about 10 to 15 minutes when using frozen fruit. Strawberry rhubarb pie in November will brighten the gloomiest of cold rainy days!

Apricot Pie

1 recipe Double Crust Pastry
  (page 32)

6 ½ cups (1.6 L) apricots, cut
  in half or quartered

¾ cup (180 mL) granulated
  sugar

3 Tbsp. (45 mL) cornstarch

1 Tbsp. (15 mL) lemon juice

½ tsp. (2.5 mL) ground
  cinnamon

1 Tbsp. (15 mL) orange zest

½ tsp. (2.5 mL) almond
  extract

1 egg beaten with 1 Tbsp.
  (15 mL) cold water

1 Tbsp. (15 mL) granulated
  sugar

¼ cup (60 mL) apricot jam,
  warmed

Was there ever a more perfect fruit than the apricot? Its romantic lineage (related to the rose), its charming name (the root of apricot is precocious), and endless applications, from jam to pilaf, make the apricot one of my all-time favorite fruits. But the clincher is the fact that they are so near and dear to my husband's heart. Years ago David hopefully planted an apricot pit in his mother's backyard in El Paso, Texas. The sheer power of his optimism caused that apricot seed to grow, flower and produce huge amounts of fruit. David, who does not bake (ever), called me from Texas when visiting his parents one summer and asked for the recipe for apricot pie. Even he couldn't eat all the fruit from that tree and could not bear to see it go to waste. I just wish I could have tasted a slice of that pie!

Prepare the pastry as directed, setting aside the smaller disk. Preheat the oven to 400°F (200°C).

In a large bowl mix together the apricots, ¾ cup (180 mL) sugar, cornstarch, lemon juice, cinnamon, orange zest and almond extract. Turn into the prepared crust, leaving room at the edges for sealing and crimping the pastry.

On a lightly floured board roll out the remaining disk of dough into a circle ⅛ inch (.3 cm) thick. Cut into ten ½-inch

(1.2-cm) strips using a knife or decorative crimper. Weave a lattice, beginning at the center of the pie. Trim the strips, seal and flute the edges. Brush with the egg wash and sprinkle with the 1 Tbsp. (15 mL) sugar.

If time allows, chill for 30 minutes. Bake for 10 minutes and then reduce the temperature to 350°F (175°C). Bake for 50 to 60 minutes, until the crust is golden and the filling is bubbling in the center. Cool for 2 hours before brushing on the warm apricot jam (strain if necessary). Serve warm or at room temperature. Store lightly covered at room temperature for up to 2 days.

VARIATION

PEACH PIE: Replace the apricots with peeled and sliced peaches; reduce the sugar to ⅔ cup (160 mL). Cut the top pastry into ten ¾-inch (1.8-cm) strips and omit the apricot glaze.

Peach Melba Pie

Makes one 10-inch (25-cm) pie (serves 8)

1 recipe Double Crust Pastry
(page 32)
4½ cups (1.1 L) peeled and
sliced fresh peaches
2 cups (475 mL) raspberries
⅔ cup (160 mL) granulated
sugar
3 Tbsp. (45 mL) cornstarch
1 Tbsp. (15 mL) lemon juice
1 Tbsp. (15 mL) orange zest
½ tsp. (2.5 mL) almond
extract
1 egg, beaten with 1 Tbsp.
(15 mL) cold water
¼ cup (60 mL) butter, cut
into ½-inch (1.2-cm) pieces
½ cup (120 mL) granulated
sugar
½ cup (120 mL) all-purpose
flour
½ cup (120 mL) sliced
almonds

This pie was inspired by a peach and raspberry dessert created by the famous French chef Auguste Escoffier in honor of Australian opera singer Nellie Melba. Although perfect on their own, plump peaches take on a whole new charm when paired with lush, fragrant raspberries. Like most berries, raspberries are usually very runny when hot, so cool this pie for two to three hours before cutting. (Unless, of course, you want to use a spoon. Not a bad idea—get a bowl, some ice cream and go for it!)

Prepare the pastry as directed, setting aside the smaller disk. Preheat the oven to 400°F (200°C).

Place the peaches in a medium bowl and the raspberries in a smaller bowl. Divide the ⅔ cup (160 mL) sugar between the two bowls, adding ½ cup (120 mL) to the peaches and the rest to the raspberries. Divide the cornstarch between the two bowls, adding 2 Tbsp. (30 mL) to the peaches and 1 Tbsp (15 mL) to the raspberries. Add the lemon juice, orange zest and almond extract to the peaches, mixing well. Turn the peaches into the prepared crust, pushing them to the sides, but leaving room at the edges for sealing and crimping the pastry. Stir the raspberries and pour into the center.

On a lightly floured board roll out the remaining disk of dough into a circle ⅛ inch (.3 cm) thick. Cut it into ten ⅔-inch (1.6-cm) strips using a knife or decorative crimper. Weave a lattice, beginning at the center of the pie. Trim the strips, seal and flute the edges. Brush with egg wash.

To make the topping, combine the butter, ½ cup (120 mL) sugar and flour in a small bowl. Using your fingertips, crumble the mixture until it resembles coarse meal (or combine with a food processor). Spread the topping over the pie and sprinkle the sliced almonds over top.

If time allows, chill for 30 minutes. Bake for 10 minutes, reduce the oven temperature to 350°F (175°C) and bake for 50 to 60 minutes, or until it's bubbly in the center. Serve slightly warm or at room temperature. Store lightly covered at room temperature for up to 2 days.

True Rhubarb Pie

Makes one 10-inch (25-cm) pie (serves 8)

1 recipe Double Crust Pastry
  (page 32)
6½ cups (1.6 L) rhubarb
1 cup (240 mL) granulated
  sugar
3 Tbsp. (45 mL) cornstarch
1 tsp. (5 mL) ground
  cinnamon
½ tsp. (2.5 mL) almond
  extract
1 Tbsp. (15 mL) orange zest
1 egg beaten with 1 Tbsp.
  (15 mL) cold water
2 Tbsp. (30 mL) butter
¼ cup (60 mL) brown sugar
¼ cup (60 mL) all-purpose
  flour

Some people don't like rhubarb and never will. For the rest of us there is nothing quite like the fragrant, tart simplicity of an all-rhubarb pie. This recipe is for the purists—those of us who love the vivid, assertive personality of rhubarb. The tartness can be mellowed by the addition of a sour cream custard, producing a gorgeous rosy filling (especially if using the red Valentine variety of rhubarb), but for the truly ardent lovers of rhubarb, all that is needed to enhance the flavor is a dash of cinnamon, a bit of orange zest and a hint of almond extract. The sweet crumble topping provides a bit of contrast to the sharp tartness of the filling.

Prepare the pastry as directed, setting aside the smaller disk. Preheat the oven to 400°F (200°C).

In a large bowl mix together the rhubarb, granulated sugar, cornstarch, cinnamon, almond extract and orange zest. Turn into the prepared crust, leaving room at the edges for sealing and crimping the pastry. On a lightly floured board roll out the remaining disk of dough into a circle ⅛ inch (.3 cm) thick. Cut it

into ten ¾-inch (1.8-cm) strips using a knife or decorative crimper. Weave a lattice, beginning at the center of the pie. Trim the strips, seal and flute the edges. Brush with the egg wash.

To make the topping, combine the butter, brown sugar and flour. Using your fingertips, crumble the mixture until it resembles coarse meal (or combine with a food processor). Sprinkle the topping over the pie.

If time allows, chill for 30 minutes. Bake for 10 minutes, reduce the temperature to 350°F (175°C) and bake for 50 to 60 minutes, until the crust is golden and the filling is bubbling in the center. Serve slightly warm or at room temperature. Store lightly covered at room temperature for up to 2 days.

VARIATION

SOUR CREAM RHUBARB PIE: Decrease the rhubarb to 5½ cups (1.4 L) and add ¾ cup (180 mL) sour cream and 1 egg.

Frozen Fruit

Individually quick frozen (IQF) fruit is a real boon for the pie maker. As far as I am concerned, even though there is absolutely nothing finer in this world than a pie made from local fruit in season, a pie made from frozen fruit can come close. Frozen wild blueberries make a better pie than a box of well-traveled cultured berries. Just be sure to use unsweetened loose pieces of frozen fruit, not the sweetened variety. Measure the fruit while it is still frozen because as it melts it will be-come mushy and compacted, and your measurement will be off. After measuring, allow the fruit to thaw slightly before using, but not so long that it starts to lose its shape. Bake as for fresh fruit, increasing the baking time by 10 to 15 minutes.

Rustic Pear Pie

Makes one 10-inch (25-cm) pie (serves 8)

1 recipe Double Crust Pastry
    (page 32)
6 ½ cups (1.6 L) peeled pears,
    cut into 1-inch (2.5-cm)
    pieces
3 Tbsp. (45 mL) granulated
    sugar
3 Tbsp. (45 mL) cornstarch
1 Tbsp. (15 mL) lemon juice
½ tsp. (2.5 mL) ground
    cinnamon
pinch cloves
½ cup (120 mL) pecans
¼ cup (60 mL) raisins
⅔ cup (160 mL) brown sugar
2 Tbsp. (30 mL) butter
1 egg beaten with 1 Tbsp.
    (15 mL) cold water
1 Tbsp. (15 mL) granulated
    sugar

Pears, pears, wonderful pears! This simple homey pie was inspired by a more labor-intensive puff pastry pear dumpling I made a number of years ago for a special occasion. The combination of flaky pastry, crunchy caramelized pecans and sweet mellow pears was so perfect that I wanted to make a pie that captured the flavors and textures but was easier to prepare. Serve it warm in pretty bowls with unsweetened cream poured over the top.

Prepare the pastry as directed, but pat it into a single disk and chill for at least 20 minutes. Allow the dough to warm slightly at room temperature if it is too hard to roll. On a lightly floured board roll the disk to a thickness of ⅛ inch (.3 cm). Cut a circle about 4 inches (10 cm) larger than the pie plate and transfer the pastry carefully into the plate by folding in half or by rolling it onto the rolling pin. The pastry will be considerably larger than the plate.

Preheat the oven to 400°F (200°C). Combine the pears, 3 Tbsp. (45 mL) granulated sugar, cornstarch, lemon juice, cinnamon and cloves and mix thoroughly. Spoon the filling into the crust, mounding it into the center. Sprinkle with the pecans, raisins and brown sugar, and dot with the butter. Carefully fold the pastry over the filling, pleating it nicely and leaving a 3- to 4-inch (7.5- to 10-cm) area open in the center. Brush the crust with egg wash and sprinkle with the 1 Tbsp. (15 mL) sugar.

If time allows, refrigerate for 30 minutes. Bake for 10 minutes, reduce the heat to 350°F (175°C) and bake for 50 to 60 more minutes, until the crust is golden and the filling is bubbling in the center. Serve warm or at room temperature. Store lightly covered at room temperature for up to 2 days.

Pear Cranberry Pie

Makes one 10-inch (25-cm) pie (serves 8)

1 recipe Double Crust Pastry
   (page 32)
5 cups (1.2 L) peeled and
   cored pears, cut into 1-inch
   (2.5-cm) pieces
1 ½ cups (360 mL) cranberries
¾ cup (180 mL) granulated
   sugar
3 Tbsp. (45 mL) cornstarch
1 Tbsp. (15 mL) lemon juice
1 Tbsp. (15 mL) orange zest
1 egg beaten with 1 Tbsp.
   (15 mL) cold water
¼ cup (60 mL) butter, cut
   into ½-inch (1.2-cm) pieces
½ cup (120 mL) granulated
   sugar
½ cup (120 mL) all-purpose
   flour

It's time to give pears their due. For some reason they are passed over in favor of apples in so many recipes, when pears can have so much to offer. The amazing color, fragrance and mellow flavor of a perfectly ripe pear is the stuff of poetry. In this pie the intense tartness and vivid color of cranberries is a perfect match for the subtle sweetness and tender texture of pears. A hint of orange and a sweet crumbly streusel topping make this a perfect fall pie.

Prepare the pastry as directed, setting aside the smaller disk. Preheat the oven to 400°F (200°C).

In a large bowl, combine the pears, cranberries, the ¾ cup (180 mL) sugar, cornstarch, lemon juice and orange zest. Turn into the prepared crust, leaving room at the edges for sealing and crimping the pastry.

On a lightly floured board, roll out the remaining disk of dough into a circle ⅛ inch (.3 cm) thick. Cut it into ten ¾-inch (1.8-cm) strips using a knife or decorative crimper. Weave a lattice, beginning at the center of the pie. Trim the strips, seal and flute the edges. Brush with the egg wash.

In a small bowl, combine the butter, the ½ cup (120 mL) sugar and flour. Use your fingertips to crumble the mixture until it resembles coarse meal (or combine with a food processor). Sprinkle the topping over the pie.

If time allows, chill for 30 minutes. Bake for 10 minutes and then reduce the oven temperature to 350°F (175°C) and bake for 50 to 60 minutes or until it's bubbly in the center. Serve slightly warm or at room temperature. Store lightly covered at room temperature for up to 2 days.

Raisin Pie

1 recipe Double Crust Pastry
(page 32)

2 cups (475 mL) raisins

1 ¼ cups (300 mL) granulated
sugar

2 cups (475 mL) fresh orange
juice

2 Tbsp. (30 mL) cornstarch

¼ tsp. (1.2 mL) salt

2 tsp. (10 mL) lemon zest

2 Tbsp. (30 mL) butter

3 Tbsp. (45 mL) fresh lemon
juice

1 egg beaten with 1 Tbsp.
(15 mL) cold water

1 Tbsp. (15 mL) granulated
sugar

This is quintessentially Canadian—I have rarely come across any recipes in American cookbooks that are quite like the versions found in so many older Canadian collections. At first I wasn't too keen to try one, it seemed so sweet and cloying, but I was pleasantly surprised. The sharp flavor of the citrus juice and the richness of the butter make this simple traditional pie a delightful treat.

Prepare the pastry as directed, setting aside the smaller disk. Preheat the oven to 400°F (200°C).

Combine the raisins, sugar, orange juice, cornstarch and salt in a medium saucepan. Simmer over medium heat until bubbly and slightly thickened, about 5 minutes. The mixture will seem thin, but the raisins will absorb the liquid. Remove from the heat. Stir in the lemon zest, butter and lemon juice. Cool completely.

Turn the cooled filling into the prepared crust, leaving room at the edges for sealing and crimping the top pastry. On a lightly floured board, roll out the remaining disk of dough into a circle $\frac{1}{8}$ inch (.3 cm) thick. Cut it into ten $\frac{3}{4}$-inch (1.8-cm) strips using a knife or decorative crimper. Weave a lattice, beginning at the center of the pie. Trim the strips, seal and flute the edges. Brush with the egg wash and sprinkle with the 1 Tbsp. (15 mL) sugar.

If time allows, chill for 30 minutes. Bake for 10 minutes, reduce the temperature to 350°F (175°C) and bake for 50 to 60 minutes, until the crust is golden and the filling is bubbling in the center. Serve slightly warm or at room temperature. Store lightly covered at room temperature for up to 3 days.

Tarte Tatin

Makes one 10-inch (25-cm) tarte (serves 8)

¾ cup (180 mL) granulated sugar

1 Tbsp. (15 mL) lemon juice

2 Tbsp. (30 mL) water

¼ cup (60 mL) butter, cut into ½-inch (1.2-cm) pieces

1 tsp. (5 mL) vanilla extract

10 cups (2.5 L) apples (about 8 medium) peeled and cut into ½-inch (1.2-cm) wedges

1 recipe Single Crust Pastry (page 31)

Don't be afraid to try this traditional French dessert—it is actually a simple upside-down apple pie. Caramelizing the sugar and pre-cooking the apples before baking enhances the flavor and firmness of the fruit and gives a lovely golden color to the finished pie. Pears work equally as well in this tarte, and peaches or plums can be used as long as they are firm and not overly ripe and juicy.

Combine the sugar, lemon juice and water in a 10-inch (25-cm) cast iron skillet. Cook over medium heat, stirring often until the mixture comes to a boil. Reduce heat to low and cook without stirring until the liquid turns a deep golden color, about 10 to 15 minutes. Remove from the heat and stir in the butter and vanilla. Arrange a single layer of apples over the caramel in a decorative fashion. Layer the remaining apples evenly in the skillet. Cook over medium-low heat, basting until the syrup becomes thick, about 20 to 30 minutes. Remove from the heat and cool for about 30 minutes.

Preheat the oven to 400°F (200°C). Prepare the pastry as directed, but when you roll it out, roll it about 1 inch (2.5 cm) larger than the skillet, cutting away the excess dough. Set the pastry on top of the apples and push the edges down inside the pan. Bake for 20 to 30 minutes or until the pastry is golden. Cool for 10 to 15 minutes. Place a plate over the crust and invert the tart carefully. Serve warm with whipped cream or ice cream.

VARIATIONS

PEAR OR PEACH TARTE TATIN: Add a pinch of cloves to the pears. Replace the vanilla with ½ tsp. (2.5 mL) almond extract for peaches.

Linzertorte

¾ cup (180 mL) butter, softened

1 cup (240 mL) granulated sugar

2 eggs

1 tsp. (5 mL) lemon zest

1 ½ cups (360 mL) all-purpose flour

1 ½ cups (360 mL) finely ground almonds

½ tsp. (2.5 mL) ground cinnamon

½ tsp. (2.5 mL) ground cloves

1 Tbsp. (15 mL) cocoa

¼ tsp. (1.2 mL) salt

1 tsp. (5 mL) baking powder

1 cup (240 mL) raspberry jam

In my early twenties, while in Switzerland for a number of months, I sampled this dessert every chance I got and I still vivdly remember the first time I tasted it. Serve it warm or at room temperature to best appreciate its unique texture. Use a homemade or premium quality raspberry jam for this recipe.

Preheat the oven to 350°F (175°C). Butter a 10 x 1¼-inch (25 x 3-cm) springform pan or tart pan with a removable bottom and line it with parchment paper.

Using an electric mixer, cream the butter and sugar until light, about 2 minutes. Add the eggs one at a time, beating until the mixture is light and fluffy, about 2 minutes. Stir in the lemon zest. In a separate bowl, combine the flour, almonds, cinnamon, cloves, cocoa, salt and baking powder. Add to the egg mixture, beating until smooth. Press ⅔ of the mixture into the bottom and sides of the prepared tart pan. Chill for 20 to 30 minutes. Spread the jam over the dough. Using a pastry bag with a wide nozzle, pipe the remaining dough in a lattice pattern over the jam. Bake for 30 to 40 minutes, until set and golden. Cool for at least 1 hour before removing from the pan to a serving plate. Store lightly covered at room temperature for up to 5 days, or refrigerated for up to 10 days.

Seasonal Fruit Cobbler

Serves 12

6 cups (1.5 L) sliced fresh
   peaches or nectarines
3 cups (720 mL) fresh strawberries, sweet cherries or
   other sweet berries
¾ cup (180 mL) packed
   brown sugar
2 Tbsp. (30 mL) cornstarch
2 Tbsp. (30 mL) orange juice
1 Tbsp. (15 mL) orange zest
2 cups (475 mL) all-purpose
   flour
⅔ cup (160 mL) granulated
   sugar
1 Tbsp. (15 mL) baking
   powder
¼ tsp. (1.2 mL) salt
½ cup (120 mL) cold butter,
   cut into ½-inch (1.2-cm)
   pieces
1 cup (240 mL) whipping
   cream
½ tsp. (2.5 mL) almond
   extract

You can't miss with this absolutely effortless recipe—a gorgeous celebration of the bounty of summer's harvest. The freshness and quality of the fruit is of utmost importance; just be sure to include fruits with some substance, such as peaches, pears or nectarines. There is no bottom crust to worry about and the rich biscuit topping takes only minutes in the food processor. Pop it in the oven just before dinner and serve it hot with vanilla ice cream or sweetened whipped cream for dessert. What could be easier?

Preheat the oven to 375°F (190°C). Butter a 9 x 12-inch (23 x 30-cm) baking dish.

Combine the fruit, brown sugar, cornstarch, orange juice and zest. Pour into the prepared dish.

Using a food processor or pastry cutter, combine the flour, granulated sugar, baking powder and salt. Cut in the butter until the mixture resembles coarse meal. Add the whipping cream and almond extract. Stir briefly until the mixture is no longer dry and powdery and is just beginning to clump. Spoon over the fruit.

Bake for 50 to 60 minutes, until the top is golden and the fruit is bubbly. Serve warm.

Plum Kuchen

Makes one 9-inch (23-cm) cake (serves 8)

FOR THE PASTRY:

½ cup (120 mL) cold butter, cut into ½-inch (1.2-cm) pieces

1 ½ cups (360 mL) all-purpose flour

3 Tbsp. (45 mL) brown sugar

1 tsp. (5 mL) ground cinnamon

¼ tsp. (1.2 mL) ground cloves

¼ tsp. (1.2 mL) salt

3 Tbsp. (45 mL) sour cream

FOR THE FILLING:

2 Tbsp. (30 mL) toasted breadcrumbs

3 ½ cups (840 mL) Italian prune plums, halved and pitted

⅓ cup (80 mL) sour cream

⅞ cup (210 mL) granulated sugar

3 egg yolks

1 Tbsp. (15 mL) all-purpose flour

2 tsp. (10 mL) vanilla extract

Kuchen simply means "cake" in German and this traditional plum cake made with Italian prune plums bakes up fragrant, moist and gorgeously purple. Serve it warm with vanilla ice cream.

FOR THE PASTRY: Preheat the oven to 350°F (175°C). Using a food processor or pastry cutter, cut in the butter, flour, 1 Tbsp. (15 mL) of the brown sugar, cinnamon, cloves, salt and sour cream until the mixture is mealy. Reserve ½ cup (120 mL) of the mixture and press the remainder into the bottom and up the sides of a 9-inch (23-cm) springform cake pan. Add the remaining 2 Tbsp. (30 mL) brown sugar to the reserved pastry mixture and blend in with your fingertips until crumbly. Set aside.

FOR THE FILLING: Sprinkle the breadcrumbs over the prepared crust. Place the plums over top in an attractive pattern. Mix together the sour cream, granulated sugar, egg yolks, flour and vanilla. Pour over the plums and sprinkle with the reserved pastry crumble.

Bake for about 60 to 70 minutes. Serve slightly warm or at room temperature. Store lightly covered in the refrigerator for up to 3 days.

Torta Rustica

FOR THE BATTER:

¾ cup (180 mL) butter, softened

1 cup (240 mL) granulated
sugar

1 Tbsp. (15 mL) orange zest

½ tsp. (2.5 mL) vanilla
extract

1 egg

2 egg yolks

¾ cup (180 mL) all-purpose
flour

¾ cup (180 mL) cornmeal

2 tsp. (10 mL) baking powder

¼ tsp. (1.2 mL) salt

¼ cup (60 mL) milk

FOR THE TOPPING:

4 cups (950 mL) peeled pears,
cut into wedges

⅓ cup (80 mL) granulated
sugar

½ cup (120 mL) chopped
walnuts

2 Tbsp. (30 mL) butter,
melted

½ cup (120 mL) apricot jam

This super-moist dessert is a version of a traditional Italian cake found in as many incarnations as there are villages in Italy. Pears are customary but it works equally well with apricots, peaches or plums. The unique taste, color and texture of this cake come from the addition of cornmeal to the rich batter. When served slightly warm, it is irresistible.

FOR THE BATTER: Preheat the oven to 350°F (175°C). Butter and flour a 10-inch (25-cm) springform pan.

Using an electric mixer or a wooden spoon, cream the butter and sugar until light and fluffy. Beat in the orange zest and vanilla. Add the egg and egg yolks one at a time, beating very well after each addition. Combine the flour, cornmeal, baking powder and salt. Add half the dry ingredients to the batter, then the milk, then the remaining dry ingredients. Spread the batter in the prepared pan.

FOR THE TOPPING: Arrange the fruit decoratively over the batter. Sprinkle the sugar and nuts over top and drizzle with the melted butter.

Bake for 50 to 60 minutes, until golden. Melt the apricot jam, straining it if necessary, and brush over the warm cake. Serve slightly warm or at room temperature. Store lightly covered at room temperature for up to 2 days.

Cherry Clafouti

2 Tbsp. (30 mL) butter, softened

5 eggs

⅔ cup (160 mL) granulated sugar

2 tsp. (10 mL) vanilla extract

½ tsp. (2.5 mL) almond extract

1¾ cups (420 mL) milk

2 Tbsp. (30 mL) amaretto or kirsch

¾ cup (180 mL) all-purpose flour

3½ cups (840 mL) pitted sweet cherries

¼ cup (60 mL) icing sugar

Clafouti is a traditional specialty from France originally made with sweet cherries, unpitted for added flavor, baked in a rich, sweet egg mixture somewhere between a custard and a pancake batter. Other firm fruits, such as plums and apricots, can be used but it's hard to improve on the original (although I feel sour cherries are even more wonderful—just sprinkle on a bit more sugar when you're serving it).

Preheat the oven to 425°F (220°C). Spread the softened butter in a heavy 10-inch (25-cm) cake pan or baking dish.

Using an electric mixer or metal whisk, beat the eggs, granulated sugar, vanilla, almond extract, milk and liqueur until combined, about 2 to 3 minutes. Add the flour and mix until smooth. Pour the batter into the prepared pan and sprinkle the cherries over the top. Bake for about 30 minutes, or until set when lightly pressed in the center. Sprinkle with the icing sugar and serve warm.

Apricot Frangipane Tarte

Makes one 10-inch (25-cm) tart (serves 10 to 12)

FOR THE CRUST:

¾ cup (180 mL) cold butter, cut into ½-inch (1.2-cm) pieces

2 cups (475 mL) all-purpose flour

¼ tsp. (1.2 mL) salt

⅓ cup (80 mL) granulated sugar

4 Tbsp. (60 mL) water

FOR THE POACHED APRICOTS:

1½ cups (360 mL) water

¾ cup (180 mL) granulated sugar

8 to 12 fresh apricots

The sweet mild taste of almonds is a natural match for tart, assertive apricots. The ground almond filling puffs up crispy and golden around the tender juicy apricots. Glistening and fragrant, this dessert makes the most of summer's bounty.

FOR THE CRUST: Using a food processor or pastry blender, combine the butter, flour, salt and sugar. Process until the mixture resembles coarse meal. Add the water and combine until the dough just comes together. Press into a disk, wrap in plastic and chill until firm, about 20 to 30 minutes.

Roll the dough into a 12-inch (30-cm) circle. Fit into a 10 x 1¼-inch (25 x 3-cm) flan pan with a removable bottom. Repair any cracks by pressing firmly. Trim the edges and press them up slightly so they rise about ⅛ inch (.3 cm) above the top of the pan. Chill for 20 minutes.

FOR THE POACHED APRICOTS: In a medium saucepan, combine the water and sugar. Bring to a boil and simmer for 3 minutes. Place the apricots in the syrup and cook until tender, about 15 minutes. Cool. Cut the apricots in half and discard the pits. Reserve the poaching liquid.

FOR THE FILLING:

1¼ cups (300 mL) blanched almonds

2 Tbsp. (30 mL) granulated sugar

½ cup (120 mL) butter, softened

½ cup (120 mL) granulated sugar

1 egg

1 egg yolk

¼ cup (60 mL) brandy or rum

2 Tbsp. (30 mL) all-purpose flour

½ tsp. (2.5 mL) almond extract

1 tsp. (5 mL) vanilla extract

1 tsp. (5 mL) lemon zest

1 Tbsp. (15 mL) butter, melted

2 Tbsp. (30 mL) granulated sugar

FOR THE GLAZE:

1 Tbsp. (15 mL) brandy or rum

FOR THE FILLING: Preheat the oven to 375°F (190°C). Combine the almonds and 2 Tbsp. (30 mL) sugar in a food processor. Process until powdery. Using an electric mixer, cream the butter and ½ cup (120 mL) sugar until light, about 2 minutes. Add the egg, egg yolk, processed almonds, brandy or rum, flour, almond extract, vanilla extract and lemon zest. Beat until well combined. Spread in the chilled tart shell. Press the cooled apricot halves into the filling in a decorative design. Brush with the melted butter and sprinkle with the remaining 2 Tbsp. (30 mL) sugar. Bake for 40 to 45 minutes. Cool.

FOR THE GLAZE: Bring the reserved poaching liquid to a boil and simmer until thick and syrupy, about 15 minutes. Measure out ¾ cup (180 mL). Stir in the brandy or rum. Brush over the cooled tart. Serve at room temperature. Store refrigerated in a covered container for up to 3 days.

Baked Custard Pies

Custard pies have a special charm of their own—they are soothing, old-fashioned and wonderfully easy to make. From the homey pumpkin to the sophisticated tarte au citron, there is a custard pie for every occasion. Since I am a great fan of all kinds of nuts—almonds, pecans and walnuts in particular—I usually favor those custard pies that have the added crunch and texture of nuts, and several of my personal favorites are in this chapter. Certainly no collection of custard pies can be complete without some of the sentimental classics, such as pecan, chocolate and everyone's number-one choice: pumpkin!

Pecan Pie

Makes one 10-inch (25-cm) pie (serves 8 to 10)

FOR THE CRUST:

½ cup (120 mL) cold butter, cut into ½-inch (1.2-cm) pieces

1¼ cups (300 mL) all-purpose flour

½ cup (120 mL) granulated sugar

¼ tsp. (1.2 mL) salt

1¼ cups (300 mL) pecan pieces

2 Tbsp. (30 mL) water

FOR THE FILLING:

4 eggs

½ cup (120 mL) granulated sugar

¾ cup (180 mL) brown sugar

½ tsp. (2.5 mL) salt

⅔ cup (160 mL) corn syrup

⅔ cup (160 mL) whipping cream

1 tsp. (5 mL) vanilla extract

⅓ cup (80 mL) brandy

¼ cup (60 mL) butter, melted

1½ cups (360 mL) pecan halves

This version of pecan pie is rich without being as sweet as most. The filling takes no time to prepare and the pecan crust is even easier; it needs no rolling and prebakes without puffing up. A plain shortbread crust would also work very well, but I prefer the crunchiness that the chopped nuts add to the overall texture of the pie.

FOR THE CRUST: Preheat the oven to 375°F (190°C). In a food processor, combine the butter, flour, sugar, salt and pecans. Process until the mixture is very finely chopped and beginning to clump. Add the water and process briefly. Press into a 10 x 1¼-inch (25 x 3-cm) flan pan with a removable bottom. Chill for 20 minutes. Bake for 15 minutes until just set. Reduce the oven temperature to 350°F (175°C).

FOR THE FILLING: Using an electric mixer or whisk, beat the eggs, both sugars, salt and syrup until combined but not frothy. Stir in the whipping cream, vanilla, brandy, melted butter and pecans. Pour into the prepared crust. Bake for 50 to 60 minutes, or until the pastry is golden and the filling is set and slightly puffed in the center. Cool completely before serving. Store refrigerated for up to 5 days.

Ontario Sour Cherry Pie,
page 36

Pear Cranberry Pie
page 51

Sweet Potato Praline Pie
page 70

Black Bottom Chocolate Pecan Pie,
page 65

Black Bottom Chocolate Pecan Pie

Makes one 10-inch (25-cm) pie (serves 10 to 12)

FOR THE CRUST:

1 recipe Single Crust Pastry
  (page 31)

FOR THE FILLING:

4 eggs

½ cup (120 mL) granulated
  sugar

¾ cup (180 mL) brown sugar

½ tsp. (2.5 mL) salt

⅔ cup (160 mL) corn syrup

⅔ cup (160 mL) whipping
  cream

1 tsp. (5 mL) vanilla extract

⅓ cup (80 mL) brandy

¼ cup (60 mL) butter, melted

1 ½ cups (360 mL) pecan
  halves

FOR THE TOPPING:

½ cup (120 mL) whipping
  cream

4 oz. (120 g) semisweet chocolate, coarsely chopped

1 Tbsp. (15 mL) corn syrup

This pie has everything—it is bittersweet, gooey, crunchy and very rich. The only thing it lacks is restraint. A customer at our Wanda's Pie in the Sky café in Toronto came in regularly for a slice of this pie. This in itself was not unusual; it is one of our most popular pies. What impressed me was the double espresso he always drank with it and the fact that it wasn't even 9:00 a.m.! That would certainly kick-start your day!

FOR THE CRUST: Preheat the oven to 375°F (190°C). Prepare the pastry as directed. Cool completely before filling.

FOR THE FILLING: Reduce the oven temperature to 350°F (175°C). Using an electric mixer or whisk, beat the eggs, both the sugars, salt and syrup until combined but not frothy. Stir in the whipping cream, vanilla, brandy, melted butter and pecans. Pour into the prepared crust. Bake for 50 to 60 minutes, until the filling is set and slightly puffed in the center. Cool completely before topping.

FOR THE TOPPING: Place a small saucepan over medium heat, and cook the cream until bubbly. Remove from the heat, stir in the chocolate and let sit for 10 minutes. Add the corn syrup and stir until smooth. Allow to cool until slightly thickened but still very shiny.

Using a teaspoon, dot the topping over the cooled pie and swirl decoratively. Serve at room temperature or slightly chilled. Store refrigerated for up to 5 days.

Tarte au Citron

Makes one 10-inch (25-cm) tart (serves 8 to 10)

FOR THE CRUST:
1 cup (240 mL) cold butter, cut into ½-inch (1.2-cm) pieces

2 cups (475 mL) all-purpose flour

⅓ cup (80 mL) cornstarch

¼ tsp. (1.2 mL) salt

¼ cup (60 mL) granulated sugar

¼ cup (60 mL) cold water

FOR THE FILLING:
8 eggs

1¾ cups (420 mL) granulated sugar

½ tsp. (2.5 mL) vanilla extract

½ tsp. (2.5 mL) almond extract

1 cup (240 mL) fresh lemon juice

1 Tbsp. (15 mL) lemon zest

½ cup (120 mL) butter

1 cup (240 mL) sliced blanched almonds

The juice and zest of lemons add so much to any dish, but when they are the star of the show, they are magic. This buttery, refreshing tart is elegant and easy to prepare and its deep lemon flavor and smooth richness will satisfy all lemon lovers. Serve it with fresh raspberries or a raspberry coulis.

FOR THE CRUST: Preheat the oven to 375°F (190°C). Using a food processor or pastry blender combine the butter, flour, cornstarch, salt and sugar and cut in until crumbly and beginning to clump. Add the water and combine until the mixture just comes together. Do not overprocess. Press into a 10 x 1¼-inch (25 x 3-cm) flan pan with a removable bottom. Chill for 30 minutes. Line with foil and pie weights or beans and bake for 20 minutes, until pale golden. Remove the foil and weights and cool to room temperature. Reduce the oven temperature to 350°F (175°C).

FOR THE FILLING: Using an electric mixer, beat the eggs and sugar until combined. Stir in the vanilla, almond extract, lemon juice and lemon zest. Melt the butter in a small saucepan over medium heat until bubbly. With the mixer on low, pour the hot butter slowly into the egg mixture. Mix until the butter is fully incorporated, about 1 minute. Stir in the almonds. Pour the mixture into the prepared crust (it will be very thin). Bake for 25 to 30 minutes, until the crust is golden and the filling is just set and no longer liquid in the center. Do not overbake. Cool to room temperature and then remove from the pan to a serving dish. Serve at room temperature. Store refrigerated for up to 3 days.

Lemon Zest

There is no substitute for freshly grated lemon zest. Other flavors, such as orange, vanilla and coconut, can be captured in pure oils and essences, but lemon flavoring, no matter how pure, always reminds me of furniture polish. The great thing about lemons is that they are readily available all year round, they're inexpensive and they are easy to zest.

Pumpkin Pie

Makes one 10-inch (25-cm) pie (serves 8 to 10)

FOR THE PIE:

1 recipe Single Crust Pastry (page 31)

5 eggs

½ cup (120 mL) brown sugar

½ cup (120 mL) granulated sugar

1 tsp. (5 mL) ground cinnamon

½ tsp. (2.5 mL) ground nutmeg

½ tsp. (2.5 mL) ground ginger

½ tsp. (2.5 mL) ground cloves

½ tsp. (2.5 mL) salt

2½ cups (600 mL) pumpkin purée

1¼ cups (300 mL) whole milk

½ cup (120 mL) whipping cream

FOR THE TOPPING:

½ cup (120 mL) whipping cream

½ tsp. (2.5 mL) vanilla extract

2 Tbsp. (30 mL) granulated sugar

To make a perfect pumpkin pie takes the skill of an alchemist—alchemy being the ancient art of creating gold from common substances. After all, who would think something so delicious could be created from a big mushy vegetable! Pumpkin pie is primarily a custard pie, and even though the main ingredient is pumpkin, it is a very strong flavor and should be mellowed with lots of milk, cream and eggs. This version is deliciously spicy, creamy and impossible to stop eating, even after a big holiday meal.

FOR THE PIE: Prepare the crust as directed. Chill for 20 minutes while preparing the filling. Preheat the oven to 350°F (175°C).

In a medium bowl, whisk the eggs lightly. Add the remaining pie ingredients and whisk thoroughly. Pour into the prepared crust. Bake for 55 to 65 minutes, or until the crust is golden and the filling is just set and no longer liquid in the center. Cool thoroughly before serving.

FOR THE TOPPING: Using an electric mixer, beat all the ingredients until soft peaks form. Serve with the chilled pie. Store the pie in the refrigerator for up to 3 days.

Sugar Pie

1 recipe Single Crust Pastry
  (page 31)
2 1/4 cups (535 mL) light
  brown sugar or maple sugar
1 cup (240 mL) whipping
  cream
2/3 cup (160 mL) maple syrup
1/4 cup (60 mL) butter
1 egg, beaten
2 Tbsp. (30 mL) all-purpose
  flour
1/2 tsp. (2.5 mL) salt
1 tsp. (5 mL) vanilla extract

The name says it all! This pie is a traditional French Canadian favorite. Although the recipes vary from region to region—some are made with cream and butter, some with evaporated milk, some with maple syrup—one constant remains: sugar, and lots of it! Serve it at room temperature in small wedges with fresh cream.

Prepare the pastry as directed. Chill for 20 minutes while preparing the filling. Preheat the oven to 350°F (175°C).

Combine the sugar, cream, maple syrup and butter in a medium saucepan. Cook over low heat, stirring occasionally, until the sugar is dissolved, about 10 to 15 minutes. Remove from the heat and cool for 15 minutes. Add the egg, flour, salt and vanilla and mix well. Pour into the prepared crust.

Bake for 40 to 45 minutes, or until set and slightly puffed in the center. Cool to room temperature before serving. Store at room temperature for up to 3 days.

Sweet Potato Praline Pie

Makes one 10-inch (25-cm) pie (serves 10)

FOR THE CRUST:

1 ¼ cups (300 mL) pecan pieces

1 ¼ cups (300 mL) all-purpose flour

⅔ cup (160 mL) granulated sugar

⅓ cup (80 mL) cold butter, cut into ½-inch (1.2- mL) pieces

2 ½ Tbsp. (38 mL) water

FOR THE FILLING:

5 eggs

1 cup (240 mL) brown sugar

2 tsp. (10 mL) ground cinnamon

¼ tsp. (1.2 mL) salt

2 ¼ cups (535 mL) cooked and mashed sweet potato (about 1 ¼ lb/568 g)

¾ cup (180 mL) whipping cream

1 ½ cups (360 mL) milk

1 tsp. (5 mL) vanilla extract

I love pumpkin pie but if I had to choose I would take this pie in a minute. Its creamy, spicy filling is similar to pumpkin but the crunchy pecan crust, maple nut praline and maple syrup drizzle elevate it to another level. It is both homey and sophisticated. At an elegant fundraiser in Toronto, I personally served this pie to hundreds of guests, and even though I had to twist a few arms for some people to sample it (we're talking about vegetable and dessert in one breath, after all!), the response was overwhelming—it was a runaway hit. The pie is not on our regular menu, but years later I still get hopeful requests for it.

FOR THE CRUST: Preheat the oven to 350°F (175°C). Combine the pecans, flour, sugar and butter in a food processor. Process until mealy and just beginning to clump. Add the water and process until the dough starts to come together to form a ball. Press the pastry into a 10 x 1¼-inch (25 x 3-cm) flan pan with a removable bottom. Bake for 20 minutes, until pale golden.

FOR THE FILLING: Using an electric mixer or whisk, beat the eggs, sugar, cinnamon and salt until light. Add the sweet potato, cream, milk and vanilla and beat until smooth. Pour into the prebaked crust. Bake for 35 to 45 minutes, until the crust is golden and filling is no longer liquid in the center. Cool to room temperature.

FOR THE PRALINE GARNISH:

⅓ cup (80 mL) brown sugar

½ cup (120 mL) maple syrup

2 Tbsp. (30 mL) butter

2 cups (475 mL) pecan halves

FOR THE TOPPING:

1 cup (240 mL) whipping cream

½ tsp. (2.5 mL) vanilla extract

1 Tbsp. (15 mL) granulated sugar

½ cup (120 mL) maple syrup

FOR THE PRALINE GARNISH: Reduce the oven temperature to 325°F (165°C). Butter a baking sheet and line it with parchment paper. Combine the brown sugar, maple syrup and butter in a medium-sized heavy saucepan. Cook, stirring constantly, until the sugar dissolves and the mixture is bubbling. Cook for about 2 to 3 minutes, then stir in the pecans, coating them completely with the syrup. Spread the pecans on the baking sheet. Bake for 15 to 20 minutes, turning occasionally, until dark golden. Remove from the oven and spread on a buttered plate, separating the pecans. Cool.

FOR THE TOPPING: Whip the cream with the vanilla and sugar. Serve each slice with a dollop of whipped cream, a sprinkling of pralines and a drizzle of maple syrup. Store the pie in the refrigerator for up to 3 days.

Butterscotch Chocolate Chip Pie

Makes one 10-inch (25-cm) pie (serves 8)

FOR THE PIE:

1 recipe Single Crust Pastry
(page 31)

¾ cup (180 mL) butter,
softened

3 cups (720 mL) brown sugar

3 eggs, room temperature

⅓ cup (80 mL) milk

½ cup (120 mL) whipping
cream

1 tsp. (5 mL) vanilla extract

¾ cup (180 mL) pecans,
chopped

1 cup (240 mL) semisweet
chocolate chips

FOR THE TOPPING:

1 cup (240 mL) whipping
cream

1 tsp. (5 mL) vanilla extract

2 Tbsp. (30 mL) granulated
sugar

1 recipe Hot Fudge Sauce
(page 211)

This is a little like a giant gooey chocolate chip cookie in a crust. As if it needs hot fudge sauce and whipped cream—but why stop now?

FOR THE PIE: Prepare the pastry as directed. Chill for 20 minutes while preparing the filling. Preheat the oven to 325°F (165°C).

Using an electric mixer, cream the butter and sugar. Add the eggs one at a time, beating for about 1 minute after each addition. Beat in the milk, whipping cream and vanilla, then stir in the pecans and chocolate chips. Bake for 50 to 60 minutes, or until the pie is set and slightly puffed in the center. Cool to room temperature.

FOR THE TOPPING: Whip the cream with the vanilla and sugar. Serve the cooled pie with the whipped cream and hot fudge sauce. Store the pie in the refrigerator for up to 3 days.

Walnut Caramel Tarte

Makes one 9-inch (23-cm) tart (serves 10)

FOR THE CRUST:

¾ cup (180 mL) butter, softened

½ cup (120 mL) granulated sugar

¼ tsp. (1.2 mL) salt

1 egg, slightly beaten

2 cups (475 mL) all-purpose flour

FOR THE FILLING:

1½ cups (360 mL) granulated sugar

⅓ cup (80 mL) water

1 cup (240 mL) whipping cream, heated

2¼ cups (535 mL) walnuts, coarsely chopped

2 Tbsp. (30 mL) butter

1 tsp. (5 mL) vanilla extract

TO ASSEMBLE:

1 egg yolk, beaten

1 Tbsp. (15 mL) granulated sugar

If it has caramel and nuts, I can't resist it. This tart originates in Switzerland, where I was lucky enough to visit for extended periods of time. The main ingredient in this recipe is walnuts, and they really should be absolutely fresh. If you have the time, crack your own—you'll be amazed at the difference.

FOR THE CRUST: Using an electric mixer or wooden spoon beat the butter and sugar until combined. Add the salt and egg and stir to combine. Sift in the flour. Knead to make a soft dough. Divide into ⅔ and ⅓ and press into disks. Wrap in plastic and refrigerate for 30 minutes.

FOR THE FILLING: In a heavy saucepan, combine the sugar and water. Cook over medium heat, stirring constantly, until the mixture comes to a boil. Stop stirring and cook until the sugar caramelizes to a light golden brown. Slowly pour in the hot cream, cooking over medium heat until smooth (the mixture may harden temporarily). Stir in the walnuts, butter and vanilla. Cool without stirring.

TO ASSEMBLE: Preheat the oven to 400°F (200°C).

Roll out the larger piece of dough into an 11-inch (28-cm) circle. (Let it sit at room temperature until it's soft enough to roll.) Fit it into the bottom and 1½ inches (3.8 cm) up the sides of a 9-inch (23-cm) springform pan. Trim evenly and repair any tears in the pastry by pressing the pastry together firmly. Refrigerate for 15 to 30 minutes.

Roll out the remaining dough. Trim to a 9-inch (23-cm) circle. Spread the cooled filling over the pastry in the pan. Top with the circle of dough. Brush with egg yolk and fold the edge of the bottom crust over the top crust. Pierce the top all over with a fork. Sprinkle with sugar. Bake for 30 to 40 minutes, or until golden brown. Serve at room temperature. Store the pie in the refrigerator for up to 5 days.

Cream and Mousse Pies

Unlike baked custard pies, which tend to be more tame and subtle, cream and mousse pies should always be sumptuous billowy affairs, topped with great dollops of sweetened whipped cream and mountains of meringue. Whether it is a wonderfully squishy banana cream, or a voluptuous lemon meringue, no one can resist the comforting yet sensual appeal of a cream pie.

Coconut Cream Pie

Makes one 10-inch (25-cm) pie (serves 8)

FOR THE CRUST:
1 recipe Single Crust Pastry
(page 31)

FOR THE FILLING:
½ cup (120 mL) granulated
sugar

¼ cup (60 mL) cornstarch

2¼ cups (540 mL) milk,
scalded

4 egg yolks, beaten

1 tsp. (5 mL) vanilla extract

1 cup (240 mL) flaked,
sweetened coconut

2 Tbsp. (30 mL) butter

¾ cup (180 mL) whipping
cream

This, I am proud to say, is the pie that won the World Series! Really! The year was 1992. It was the sixth game of the World Series. The place was Toronto. Toronto was ahead by three games and needed one more to clinch the championship. As all Toronto fans know, Joltin' Joe Carter hit that magical home run, winning the game and the series. So where does the coconut pie fit into all this? Joe Carter was a loyal fan of our pies and regularly ordered them. On the Friday before that fateful Saturday night game, Joe ordered a large coconut cream pie and my husband, David, rushed to the SkyDome that afternoon with pie in hand. He gave it to Joe with a proviso: "Once you win the World Series (is there any doubt?), please return the pie plate in person to our bakery." Needless to say, Joe had more important things to do after that game. To this day we maintain that our coconut cream pie gave a little lift to that ball. That's our story and we're sticking to it!

FOR THE CRUST: Prepare the pastry as directed and chill for 30 minutes. Preheat the oven to 400°F (200°C). Line the crust with foil and fill with metal pie weights or beans. Bake for 15 to 20 minutes. Carefully remove the foil and continue baking for 10 to 15 minutes, until golden. Cool completely before filling.

FOR THE FILLING: Combine the sugar and cornstarch in a heavy saucepan. Add the scalded milk and stir in thoroughly. Cook over medium-low heat, stirring constantly, until thick and smooth. Add about 1 cup (240 mL) of the hot mixture to the beaten egg yolks, combining until smooth. Whisking vigorously, add the yolks to the pot and continue cooking, stirring constantly, just until the mixture comes to a boil. Remove from the heat and stir in the vanilla, coconut and butter. Transfer to a metal bowl, cover with plastic wrap and chill in the refrigerator for at least 2 hours.

1 cup (240 mL) whipping
   cream

2 Tbsp. (30 mL) granulated
   sugar

$\frac{1}{2}$ tsp. (2.5 mL) vanilla
   extract

$\frac{1}{4}$ cup (60 mL) shredded
   sweetened coconut, toasted

Whip the cream to stiff peaks and fold into the cold filling. Mound into the pie shell. Cover with plastic wrap and chill for 3 hours.

FOR THE TOPPING: Whip the cream until soft peaks form. Add the sugar and vanilla and beat until stiff. Spoon or pipe it onto the cooled pie and sprinkle with toasted coconut. Chill until serving time. Store in the refrigerator for up to 2 days.

Banana Cream Pie

Makes one 10-inch (25-cm) pie (serves 8)

FOR THE CRUST:

1 recipe Single Crust Pastry
(page 31)

FOR THE FILLING:

½ cup (120 mL) granulated
sugar

¼ cup (60 mL) cornstarch

2¼ cups (540 mL) milk,
scalded

4 egg yolks, beaten

1 tsp. (5 mL) vanilla extract

2 Tbsp. (30 mL) butter

¾ cup (180 mL) whipping
cream

2 bananas, sliced

FOR THE TOPPING:

1 cup (240 mL) whipping
cream

½ tsp. (2.5 mL) vanilla
extract

2 Tbsp. (30 mL) sugar

1 oz. (30 g) chocolate, melted

Please don't make me choose! Not when it's between banana cream, coconut cream, lemon meringue, or chocolate cream. When it comes to cream pies, though, this one does have the edge. Believe me, I know. I've asked and banana cream lovers are the most outspoken in their preference—banana cream pie wins over lemon meringue (but just barely!). What's not to like? Mountains of whipped cream, soft, squishy custard and sweet, tender bananas, all in a flaky butter crust. Watch it disappear!

FOR THE CRUST: Prepare the pastry as directed and chill for 30 minutes. Preheat the oven to 400°F (200°C). Line the crust with foil and fill with metal pie weights or beans. Bake for 15 to 20 minutes. Carefully remove the foil and continue baking for 10 to 15 minutes, until golden. Cool completely before filling.

FOR THE FILLING: Combine the sugar and cornstarch in a heavy saucepan. Add the scalded milk and stir in thoroughly. Cook over medium-low heat, stirring constantly, until thick and smooth. Add about 1 cup (240 mL) of the hot mixture to the beaten yolks, combining until smooth. Whisking vigorously, add the yolks to the pot and continue cooking, stirring constantly, just until the mixture comes to a boil. Remove from the heat and stir in the vanilla and butter. Transfer to a metal bowl, cover with plastic wrap and chill in the refrigerator for 2 hours.

Whip the cream to stiff peaks and fold into the cold filling. Spread ⅓ of the filling in the crust and cover with half the sliced bananas. Cover with ½ of the remaining filling, the remaining bananas and a final layer of filling. Cover with plastic wrap and chill for 3 hours.

FOR THE TOPPING: Whip the cream with the vanilla and sugar. Spoon or pipe onto the cooled pie and drizzle the melted chocolate on top. Chill until serving time. Store in the refrigerator for up to 2 days.

Chocolate Cream Pie

Makes one 10-inch (25-cm) pie (serves 8)

FOR THE CRUST:
1 recipe Basic Sweet Pastry
  (page 33)

FOR THE FILLING:
3 cups (720 mL) milk
¾ cup (180 mL) granulated
  sugar
¼ cup (60 mL) cornstarch
2 Tbsp. (30 mL) all-purpose
  flour
¼ cup (60 mL) cocoa
¼ tsp. (1.2 mL) salt
5 egg yolks
5 oz. (140 g) semisweet chocolate, coarsely chopped
2 Tbsp. (30 mL) butter
2 tsp. (10 mL) vanilla extract

FOR THE TOPPING:
1½ cups (360 mL) whipping
  cream
2 Tbsp. (30 mL) granulated
  sugar
1 tsp. (5 mL) vanilla extract
chocolate curls, for garnish

One of the first things I remember cooking was a simple chocolate pudding with cornstarch, cocoa and milk. It was delicious warm or cold, although if I remember correctly, it rarely lasted long enough to be chilled. This pie truly is one of the ultimate comfort foods, and when made with the best quality cocoa and chocolate, it can be not only homey but sophisticated and elegant. The rich chocolate custard is less sweet, more intensely chocolate than most pies of this sort, satisfying even the most ardent chocolate lovers.

FOR THE CRUST: Prepare the pastry as directed, pressing the pastry into a 10-inch (25-cm) pie plate. Chill for 30 minutes. Preheat the oven to 375°F (190°C). Line the pastry with foil and fill with metal pie weights or beans. Bake for 15 minutes. Remove the foil and continue baking for 10 to 15 minutes, until golden. Cool completely before filling.

FOR THE FILLING: In a medium saucepan, heat the milk almost to a boil. Remove from the heat. Whisk together the sugar, cornstarch, flour, cocoa and salt. Add the yolks and whisk until smooth and thick. Add ½ cup (120 mL) of the hot milk, whisking until smooth. Gradually add the yolk mixture to the hot milk, whisking until smooth. Return to the heat and cook over medium-low heat, stirring with a wooden spoon, until the mixture begins to bubble. Cook for about 1 minute, stirring vigorously. Remove from the heat and stir in the chocolate, butter and vanilla. Pour the mixture through a fine mesh strainer. Pour into the prepared crust and cover with plastic wrap. Chill until cold.

FOR THE TOPPING: Using an electric mixer, beat the cream, sugar and vanilla until stiff peaks form. Mound or pipe on the pie and garnish with chocolate curls. Serve chilled. Store in the refrigerator for up to 2 days.

Peanut Butter Cream Pie

Makes one 10-inch (25-cm) pie (serves 10)

FOR THE CRUST:

¼ cup (60 mL) granulated sugar

2 oz. (57 g) semisweet chocolate, finely chopped

⅓ cup (80 mL) roasted peanuts

1¼ cups (300 mL) graham cracker crumbs

¼ cup (60 mL) butter, melted and cooled

FOR THE FILLING:

10 oz. (300 g) cream cheese, room temperature

1¼ cups (300 mL) peanut butter (smooth, not crunchy)

3 Tbsp. (45 mL) butter, softened

1⅓ cups (320 mL) icing sugar, sifted

⅔ cup (160 mL) whipping cream

1 tsp. (5 mL) vanilla extract

FOR THE TOPPING:

⅔ cup (160 mL) whipping cream

6 oz. (180 g) semisweet chocolate, finely chopped

1 Tbsp. (15 mL) corn syrup

toasted peanuts, for garnish

Make this pie when you want to make friends. Who can resist rich creamy chocolate with gooey peanut butter in a crunchy peanut-graham crust? It's really a giant candy, but isn't that the whole point of peanut butter and chocolate?

FOR THE CRUST: Preheat the oven to 350°F (175°C). Combine the sugar, chocolate and peanuts in a food processor. Process until finely chopped. Thoroughly combine the graham cracker crumbs, chopped nut/chocolate mixture and melted butter in a bowl. Press onto the bottom and sides of a 10-inch (25-cm) pie plate. Bake for 15 minutes, until golden and firm. Cool.

FOR THE FILLING: Using an electric mixer, beat the cream cheese, peanut butter and butter in a large bowl until light and fluffy. Add the icing sugar and beat until combined. Whip the cream and vanilla in a separate bowl until stiff peaks form. Fold the cream into the peanut butter mixture. Spread in the cooled crust, smoothing with a spatula. Refrigerate for at least 2 to 3 hours.

FOR THE TOPPING: Bring the cream to a slow boil in a heavy saucepan over low heat. Remove from the heat, add the chocolate and stir until smooth. Mix in the syrup. Allow to cool until it is beginning to thicken slightly but is still smooth. Pour ⅔ of the chocolate over the cooled pie, making sure it covers all the way to the edges.

Allow the remainder of the chocolate to cool to room temperature. Using a pastry bag with a small star tip, pipe a decorative edge on the pie. Garnish with whole toasted peanuts. Chill until serving time. Store in the refrigerator for up to 4 days.

Strawberry Chocolate Mousse Pie

Makes one 10-inch (25-cm) pie (serves 10)

FOR THE CRUST:

1 recipe Basic Sweet Pastry
(page 33)

FOR THE FILLING:

8 oz. (240 g) semisweet chocolate, coarsely chopped

¼ cup (60 mL) butter

1 cup (240 mL) whipping
cream

4 large eggs, separated

¼ cup (60 mL) granulated
sugar

FOR THE TOPPING:

1 cup (240 mL) whipping
cream

2 Tbsp. (30 mL) granulated
sugar

½ tsp (2.5 mL) vanilla extract

4 oz. (120 g) chocolate, finely
chopped

10 strawberries

*Strawberry chocolate mousse pie was the first "extravagant" addi-
tion to the line of Wanda's Pie in the Sky desserts. Alan Miceli, our
chief cream pie baker back then, regularly took this pie home for
birthdays and special occasions. One snowy winter afternoon, he
was preparing to leave the bakery, a large cake box in his hands.
To this day I still marvel at how he managed to carry that moun-
tain of mousse, strawberries and whipped cream home, riding
through the snow on his bicycle, one hand steering and the other
balancing his precious cargo! Pull out all the stops on this sumptuous creation and use the best chocolate you can find; it is the star of
this show and it will definitely be worth it!*

FOR THE CRUST: Prepare the pastry as directed and chill for
30 minutes. Preheat the oven to 375°F (190°C). Line the crust
with foil and fill with metal pie weights or beans. Bake for
15 minutes. Remove the foil and continue baking for 10 to
15 minutes, until golden. Cool completely before filling.

FOR THE FILLING: Melt the chocolate and butter in a medium
saucepan over low heat or in the microwave. Do not overheat.
Set aside. Whip the cream to soft peaks. Beat the egg whites to
soft peaks. In a large bowl, mix together the yolks and sugar.
Stir in the chocolate. Fold the cream into the chocolate mixture.
Fold in the egg whites. Do not overbeat, as this may deflate the
mousse. Spread into the cooled crust. Chill for 2 or 3 hours.

FOR THE TOPPING: Whip the cream until soft peaks form. Add
the sugar and vanilla and beat until stiff. Spoon or pipe onto
the cooled pie. Melt the chocolate in a double boiler over hot
water or in the microwave. Dip the strawberries halfway into
the chocolate and place around the border of the pie. Drizzle
with the remaining chocolate. Chill until serving time. Store in
the refrigerator for up to 2 days.

Fresh Fruit Custard Tarte

Makes one 10-inch (25-cm) tart (serves 10)

FOR THE CRUST:

1 recipe Basic Sweet Pastry
(page 33; increase sugar
from ⅓ cup/80 mL) to
½ cup/120 mL)

FOR THE FILLING:

1 ¾ cups (420 mL) half-and-
half

⅔ cup (160 mL) granulated
sugar

2 Tbsp. (30 mL) cornstarch

1 Tbsp. (15 mL) all-purpose
flour

pinch salt

5 egg yolks, beaten slightly

4 Tbsp. (60 mL) butter

1 tsp. (5 mL) vanilla extract

¾ cup (180 mL) heavy cream

FOR THE TOPPING:

fresh fruit (strawberries, raspberries, blueberries, kiwi,
grapes, peaches, etc.)

½ cup (120 mL) apple or
raspberry juice concentrate

2 tsp. (10 mL) cornstarch

There is no better way to showcase the freshest fruits of each sea-son than in a simple glazed tarte. Whether topped with ripe red strawberries, delicate raspberries, golden summer peaches or what-ever gorgeous berry that is in season, this fragile yet sumptuous custard tart makes a spectacular presentation.

FOR THE CRUST: Prepare the pastry as directed. Preheat the oven to 375°F (190°C). Line the pastry with foil and fill with metal pie weights or beans. Bake for 15 minutes. Remove the foil and continue baking for 10 to 15 minutes, until golden. Cool completely before filling.

FOR THE FILLING: In a medium saucepan, bring the half-and-half almost to a boil. Remove from the heat. In a medium bowl, combine the sugar, cornstarch, flour and salt. Add the yolks and whisk until smooth. Add ½ cup (120 mL) of the hot half-and-half, whisking until smooth. Gradually add the yolk mix-ture to the cream, whisking until smooth. Return to the stove and cook over medium heat, stirring with a wooden spoon, until the mixture begins to bubble. Cook for about 1 minute, stirring vigorously. Remove from the heat and stir in the butter and vanilla. Pour into a bowl and cover with plastic wrap. Chill until cold. Whip the cream until stiff peaks form. Fold into the chilled custard. Spread in the prepared crust and smooth.

FOR THE TOPPING: Cover the custard decoratively with whole and sliced fruit. Cook the fruit juice concentrate and cornstarch in a small saucepan over medium heat until the mixture comes to a simmer. Boil for ½ minute. Brush onto the fruit with a pastry brush. Best served within 2 or 3 hours.

Key Lime Pie

Makes one 9-inch (23-cm) pie (serves 6)

FOR THE CRUST:

1 cup (240 mL) graham
   cracker crumbs

⅔ cup (160 mL) sweetened
   shredded coconut

2 Tbsp. (30 mL) sugar

1 tsp. (5 mL) vanilla extract

¼ cup (60 mL) butter, melted

FOR THE FILLING:

4 egg yolks

1 14-oz (398-mL) can
   sweetened condensed milk

½ cup (120 mL) fresh lime
   juice

1 Tbsp. (15 mL) lime zest

½ tsp. (2.5 mL) vanilla
   extract

FOR THE TOPPING:

1¼ cups (300 mL) whipping
   cream

1 Tbsp. (5 mL) granulated
   sugar

½ tsp. (2.5 mL) vanilla extract
lime slices, for garnish

There are countless versions of this pie, each a little different, but the two ingredients that seem to be absolutely necessary are sweetened condensed milk and, of course, fresh limes. The Florida Key limes are less tart than the Persian limes more commonly used, and although traditional, I feel they do not necessarily make for a better pie. I've added coconut to the graham cracker crust for added tropical flavor and interest, and so that you can sing, just like Harry Neilson, "you've got to put de lime in de coconut," when you serve this pie.

FOR THE CRUST: Preheat the oven to 350°F (175°C). Using a fork, combine the graham cracker crumbs, coconut, sugar, vanilla and butter in a medium-size bowl. Press into a 9-inch (23-cm) pie plate. Bake for 15 to 20 minutes, or until golden. Cool completely before filling.

FOR THE FILLING: Using a whisk, combine the egg yolks, condensed milk, lime juice, lime zest and vanilla. Pour into the baked crust. Chill for 2 hours.

FOR THE TOPPING: Using an electric mixer, beat the cream with the sugar and vanilla until stiff peaks form. Pipe or spoon onto the chilled pie. Chill until serving time. Serve garnished with lime slices. Store in the refrigerator for up to 2 days.

Chocolate Raspberry Silk Tarte

Makes one 10-inch (25-cm) tart (serves 12)

FOR THE CRUST:

$\frac{1}{3}$ cup (80 mL) cold butter, cut into $\frac{1}{2}$-inch (1.2-cm) pieces

1 $\frac{1}{4}$ cups (300 mL) all-purpose flour

1 $\frac{1}{4}$ cups (300 mL) hazelnuts, toasted

$\frac{2}{3}$ cup (160 mL) granulated sugar

2 oz. (57 g) semisweet chocolate, coarsely chopped

1 $\frac{1}{2}$ Tbsp. (22.5 mL) water

FOR THE FILLING:

12 oz. (340 g) semisweet chocolate, coarsely chopped

$\frac{1}{2}$ cup (120 mL) butter, softened

1 cup (240 mL) icing sugar

4 eggs, room temperature

$\frac{1}{4}$ cup (60 mL) hazelnut liqueur

$\frac{3}{4}$ cup (180 mL) seedless raspberry jam

Believe it or not, even though there are quite a few steps in this gorgeous creation, none of them are difficult. No one will believe that when you present this delectable tart in all its luxurious chocolate glory. Originally I made this dessert with dried cherries and amaretto instead of raspberries and hazelnut liqueur, but since not everyone loves cherries the way I do, I've included the cherry version as a variation and am giving center stage to raspberries. Raspberries, as always, are the perfect complement to the deep dark taste of chocolate.

FOR THE CRUST: Preheat the oven to 350°F (175°C). Using a food processor, combine the butter, flour, hazelnuts, sugar and chocolate and process until mealy and just beginning to clump. Add the water and process until the dough starts to come together. Press into a 10 x 1 $\frac{1}{4}$-inch (25 x 3-cm) tart pan with a removable bottom. Chill for 15 minutes. Bake for 20 to 25 minutes, until golden. Cool completely before filling.

FOR THE FILLING: Melt the chocolate in a microwave or in a double boiler over hot water. Cool to lukewarm. Using an electric mixer, beat the butter and icing sugar until light and fluffy, about 1 to 2 minutes. Beat in the melted chocolate. Add the eggs, one at a time, beating for 1 minute after each addition. Beat in the liqueur. Spread the raspberry jam on the cooled crust and cover with the chocolate mousse. Smooth with a metal spatula. Cover lightly with plastic wrap and chill until firm.

FOR THE GLAZE:

½ cup (120 mL) whipping
cream

4 oz. (113 g) semisweet chocolate, coarsely chopped

1 Tbsp. (15 mL) corn syrup

1 Tbsp. (15 mL) hazelnut
liqueur

1 cup (240 mL) raspberries

FOR THE GLAZE: Bring the cream to a slow boil in a heavy saucepan over low heat. Remove from the heat, add the chocolate and stir until melted. Stir in the corn syrup and liqueur. Allow to cool until it is slightly thickened, but is still smooth. Pour over the chilled tart, making sure it covers all the way to the edges. (Try tilting the tart gently to allow the glaze to spread itself.) Place the raspberries around the edge of the tart. Refrigerate until serving time. Store in the refrigerator for up to 2 days.

VARIATION

CHOCOLATE CHERRY SILK TART: Substitute amaretto or kirsch for the hazelnut liqueur. For the filling, add ½ cup (120 mL) dried cherries to the liqueur and soak overnight. Add the cherries with the liqueur when making the mousse. Replace the raspberry jam with sour cherry preserves. Leave the tart unadorned, or decorate it with chocolate curls.

Chocolate Curls

The simplest way to make curls is to run a chef's knife at an angle over a slightly warmed large block of chocolate—heat the chocolate in a microwave at a low setting or leave in a warm spot (75°F–85°F/ 23°C–29°C) until it feels tacky but not soft. Bracing it against your apron, scrape at an angle of 70°–80°. Re-warm the block of chocolate if it gets too brittle. This technique will produce irregular curls. For a more controlled curl, spread melted chocolate on the back of a 13 x 18-inch (32.5 cm x 45-cm) pan to a thickness of $1/16$ of an inch (.1 cm), using an offset spatula (about 8 oz/225 g per pan). Refrigerate until hardened. Let the chocolate soften at room temperature until it is soft enough to scrape with an off-set spatula. Hold the spatula with both hands and scrape the chocolate off the pan. Depending on the angle of the spatula (10°–60°), and whether it is kept straight or bowed slightly, the curls can range from tight rolls to flat ribbons.

Lemon Meringue Pie

Makes one 10-inch (25-cm) pie (serves 8)

FOR THE CRUST:

¾ cup (180 mL) cold butter, cut into ½-inch (1.2-cm) pieces

2 cups (475 mL) all-purpose flour

¼ cup (60 mL) granulated sugar

¼ tsp. (1.2 mL) salt

⅓ cup (80 mL) water

FOR THE FILLING:

2 cups (475 mL) water

1 cup (240 mL) granulated sugar

½ cup (120 mL) cornstarch

5 egg yolks, beaten

¼ cup (60 mL) butter

¾ cup (180 mL) fresh lemon juice

1 Tbsp. (15 mL) lemon zest

1 tsp. (5 mL) vanilla extract

I don't know anyone who can resist this pie. When made correctly (tricky at first, to be sure), it is a dream come true: tart, melt-in-your-mouth filling and sweet, mile-high meringue all piled into a crispy delicate crust. I like to think of lemon meringue as the Marilyn Monroe of pies: tart, blonde, voluptuous and truly unforgettable.

FOR THE CRUST: Make sure all the ingredients are as cold as possible. Using a food processor or a pastry cutter and a large bowl, combine the butter, flour, sugar and salt. Process or cut in until the mixture resembles coarse meal and begins to clump together. Sprinkle with water, let rest for 30 seconds and then either process very briefly or cut in with about 15 strokes of the pastry cutter, just until the dough begins to stick together and come away from the sides of the bowl. Turn onto a lightly floured work surface and press together to form a disk. Wrap in plastic and chill for at least 20 minutes.

Allow the dough to warm slightly to room temperature if it is too hard to roll. On a lightly floured board roll the disk to a thickness of ⅛ inch (.3 cm). Cut a circle about 2 inches (5 cm) larger than the pie plate and transfer the pastry into the plate by folding it in half or by rolling it onto the rolling pin. Turn the pastry under, leaving an edge that hangs over the plate about ½ inch (1.2 cm). Flute decoratively. Chill for 30 minutes.

Preheat the oven to 350°F (180°C). Chill for 30 minutes. Line the crust with foil and fill with metal pie weights or beans. Bake for 20 to 25 minutes. Carefully remove the foil and continue baking for 10 to 15 minutes, until golden. Cool completely before filling.

FOR THE FILLING: Bring the water to a boil in a large, heavy saucepan. Remove from the heat and let rest for 5 minutes. Whisk the sugar and cornstarch together. Add the mixture gradually to the hot water, whisking until completely incorporated.

5 egg whites, room tem-
   perature

$\frac{1}{2}$ tsp. (2.5 mL) cream of
   tartar

$\frac{1}{4}$ tsp. (1.2 mL) salt

$\frac{1}{2}$ tsp. (2.5 mL) vanilla
   extract

$\frac{3}{4}$ cup (180 mL) granulated
   sugar

Return to the heat and cook over medium heat, whisking constantly until the mixture comes to a boil. The mixture will be very thick. Add about 1 cup (240 mL) of the hot mixture to the beaten egg yolks, whisking until smooth. Whisking vigorously, add the warmed yolks to the pot and continue cooking, stirring constantly, until the mixture comes to a boil. Remove from the heat and stir in the butter until incorporated. Add the lemon juice, zest and vanilla, stirring until combined. Pour into the prepared crust. Cover with plastic wrap to prevent a skin from forming on the surface, and cool to room temperature.

FOR THE MERINGUE: Preheat the oven to 375°F (190°C). Using an electric mixer beat the egg whites with the cream of tartar, salt and vanilla extract until soft peaks form. Add the sugar gradually, beating until it forms stiff, glossy peaks. Pile onto the cooled pie, bringing the meringue all the way over to the edge of the crust to seal it completely. Bake for 15 to 20 minutes, or until golden. Cool on a rack. Serve within 6 hours to avoid a soggy crust.

Meringue

Meringue can be tricky to perfect. Each step in preparation is vital for a successful result. The egg whites must be at room temperature and free of any fat or traces of yolk. Ensure your bowl is metal or glass and perfectly clean. Fat destroys and destabilizes the foam, producing a liquid mess. Beat the whites just until they form soft peaks, then gradually beat in sugar. Now is not the time to skimp on sugar, as it ensures a more stable meringue. Two tablespoons per egg white is a good rule of thumb. Pile the beaten meringue onto the pie immediately to maintain a smooth, silky texture and shiny peaks. To avoid weeping, caused by undercooking of the meringue, spoon the meringue on top of a room-temperature or slightly warm filling, and bake in a medium rather than hot oven. Use a hot knife and a deft hand to serve and eat within a few hours of baking.

Citrus Lace Cups

Makes 24 cups

FOR THE CUPS:

¼ cup (60 mL) butter

½ cup (120 mL) brown sugar

¼ cup (60 mL) corn syrup

½ tsp. (120 mL) vanilla
  extract

½ cup (120 mL) pastry flour

½ cup (120 mL) almonds,
  finely chopped

FOR THE FILLING:

1½ cups (360 mL) whipping
  cream, chilled

12 oz. (340 g) cream cheese,
  softened (about
  1½ packages)

1 cup (240 mL) granulated
  sugar

2 Tbsp. (30 mL) lime zest

1 tsp. (5 mL) lemon zest

1 Tbsp. (15 mL) orange zest

⅓ cup (80 mL) lime juice

2 cups (480 mL) fresh raspberries (optional)

Candied Orange Peel
  (see page 209) (optional)

You won't believe how fast and simple these scrumptious mousse-filled cups are to prepare. Believe me, I know. I personally, single-handedly prepared (well, almost single-handedly; thankfully I had some last-minute help—thank you, Sarah Jane and Sheila!) almost 700 of these fragile little miniatures for a fundraiser. I ran out of steam at about 685. I figured it would be enough, but of course it wasn't, and we had to turn away about 30 people. No doubt there would have been plenty if so many people hadn't returned for sec-onds—in some cases, thirds. Whenever you want to whip up an impressive, dazzling dessert in no time at all, be sure to give these fragile, cream-filled treats a try. You and your guests will be absolutely thrilled.

FOR THE CUPS: Preheat the oven to 375°F (190°C). Line 2 cookie sheets with parchment paper. Combine the butter, sugar and corn syrup in a medium saucepan. Bring to a boil over medium heat, stirring occasionally. Remove from the heat and stir in the vanilla. Combine the flour and almonds and add to the sugar mixture. Drop by teaspoonfuls 3 inches (7.5 cm) apart on the cookie sheets. Bake for 5 to 6 minutes, until golden brown. Remove from the pan while still hot and use a spatula to drape over the back of a mini muffin pan to create little cups. It is important to work quickly before the sugar hardens. However, if it does harden, pop the pan back into the oven for a minute to make it pliable enough to continue. Let the cups cool completely.

FOR THE FILLING: Using an electric mixer, whip the chilled cream until stiff peaks form. In a separate bowl, beat the cream cheese with the sugar, the lime, lemon and orange zests and the lime juice until light and fluffy. Gently fold in the whipped cream. Using a piping bag and star tip, pipe the filling into the cookie cups. Assemble within 20 minutes of serving to maintain crispness. Garnish the cups with raspberries or candied orange peel, if desired.

VARIATION

MARGARITA MOUSSE CUPS: Add 2 Tbsp. (30 mL) tequila and 1 Tbsp. (15 mL) Triple Sec liqueur to the beaten cream cheese for an exciting change.

Cookies

For most of us, the word cookie immediately conjures up a multitude of delightful and comforting childhood memories. We are transported to Grandma's cinnamon-scented kitchen, where we are licking the bowl and eating just-out-of-the-oven chocolate chip cookies after school. Remember actually making your first batch of cookies, all by yourself? It is remarkable how powerful and evocative a simple word can be. The sweet truth of the matter is: when it comes to cookies, fortunately most of us never grow up. We are always ready to stop and enjoy one of the simple little pleasures of life—delicious cookies. For all you kids, big and small, I've made a point of including many old-fashioned, homey recipes, just like Grandma used to make, as well as a few more elegant, sophisticated treats for those occasions when we want to pretend that we're all grown up.

Old-Fashioned Peanut Butter Cookies

Makes 2 dozen 2-inch (5-cm) cookies

½ cup (120 mL) butter,
  softened
½ cup (120 mL) brown sugar
½ cup (120 mL) granulated
  sugar
1 egg
1 tsp. (5 mL) vanilla extract
1 ¼ cups (300 mL) peanut
  butter, smooth or crunchy
¼ tsp. (1.2 mL) salt
1 ⅓ cups (320 mL) all-purpose
  flour
½ tsp. (2.5 mL) baking soda

Just one bite of this cookie—soft in the center, crispy on the edges, with its little crisscross of fork marks on the top—will transport you to the milk and cookie days of your childhood. Yes, they are as good as you remember, especially when made just right, with lots of butter, brown sugar and, of course, peanut butter. The only thing left to decide is whether to use crunchy or smooth peanut butter and whether to bake them golden crispy or soft and chewy.

Using an electric mixer or a wooden spoon, cream the butter and sugars until smooth. Add the egg, vanilla, peanut butter and salt and beat until well combined. Mix the flour and baking soda in a separate bowl and add to the peanut butter mixture. Beat until just combined. Refrigerate for 2 to 3 hours.

Preheat the oven to 325°F (165°C). Line two 18 x 12-inch (45 x 30-cm) baking sheets with parchment paper. Using a 1 ¼-inch (3-cm) ice-cream scoop or a tablespoon, roll the batter into balls about 1 inch (2.5 cm) in diameter. Place them 2 inches (5 cm) apart on the prepared pans. Use a fork to flatten the balls slightly, pressing each twice, in a crisscross pattern.

Bake for about 15 minutes, until golden brown, or 17 minutes for crispy cookies. Cool for at least 2 minutes before removing from the pans to a wire rack to cool completely. Store in a tightly closed container for up to 4 days.

Low–Fat Hermit Cookies

Makes 2 dozen 2-inch (5-cm) cookies

½ cup (120 mL) butter, softened

1 ½ cups (360 mL) dark brown sugar

2 eggs

1 tsp. (5 mL) vanilla extract

1 ¾ cups (420 mL) all-purpose flour

½ cup (120 mL) quick-cook rolled oats (not regular or instant)

½ tsp. (2.5 mL) salt

1 tsp. (5 mL) baking soda

2 tsp. (10 mL) ground cinnamon

1 tsp. (5 mL) ground nutmeg

1 ½ cups (360 mL) raisins

¾ cup (180 mL) dates, chopped

1 cup (240 mL) walnuts, chopped

Our most popular cookie—just ask our tired cookiemaker at Wanda's Pie in the Sky, who hand-scoops these darlings by the truckload. This is an old-fashioned treat, full of wholesome ingredients such as walnuts, dates, raisins, oats and spices, and it's low-fat to boot. Don't let that put you off; they are scrumptious, and since they are healthy, you can have twice as many.

Preheat the oven to 350°F (175°C). Line two 18 x 12-inch (45 x 30-cm) baking sheets with parchment paper.

Using an electric mixer or a wooden spoon, cream the butter and sugar until light and fluffy. Beat in the eggs and vanilla. Combine the flour, rolled oats, salt, baking soda, cinnamon, nutmeg, raisins, dates and walnuts in a separate bowl. Add to the butter/sugar mixture and stir to combine. Using a 1 ¼-inch (3-cm) ice-cream scoop or a tablespoon, drop the cookie dough on the prepared sheets, about 3 inches (7.5 cm) apart. Press slightly; the mixture will spread.

Bake for about 15 to 20 minutes, until set and golden brown but still soft. Cool completely before removing them from the pans. Store in a tightly closed container for up to 5 days.

Oatmeal Raisin Cookies

Makes 2 dozen 2-inch (5-cm) cookies

¾ cup (180 mL) butter

1 cup (240 mL) brown sugar

½ cup (120 mL) granulated
   sugar

1 egg

1 tsp. (5 mL) vanilla extract

1½ cups (360 mL) all-purpose
   flour

½ tsp. (2.5 mL) baking soda

¼ tsp. (1.2 mL) salt

¾ cup (180 mL) quick-cook
   rolled oats (not regular
   or instant)

1½ cups (360 mL) raisins

Don't be fooled by the name. This is nothing like the cardboard cookie in your grade-three lunch box that you couldn't swap for anything. It is so buttery, chewy and delicious that you'll forget all about chocolate.

Preheat the oven to 350°F (175°C). Line two 18 x 12-inch (45 x 30-cm) baking sheets with parchment paper.

Using an electric mixer or a wooden spoon, cream the butter and sugars until light and fluffy. Beat in the egg and vanilla. Combine the flour, baking soda, salt, rolled oats and raisins. Stir into the butter mixture. Using a 1¼-inch (3-cm) ice cream scoop or a tablespoon, drop the cookie dough on the prepared sheets, about 3 inches (7.5 cm) apart.

Bake for 12 to 15 minutes, until golden brown. Cool completely before removing from the pan. Store in a tightly closed container for up to one week.

Gorilla Cookies

Makes 3 dozen 2-inch (5-cm) cookies

1 cup (240 mL) butter,
    softened
1 ½ cups (360 mL) brown
    sugar
2 eggs
1 tsp. (5 mL) vanilla extract
1 ⅔ cups (400 mL) all-purpose
    flour
1 tsp. (5 mL) baking soda
1 tsp. (5 mL) baking powder
½ tsp. (2.5 mL) salt
1 cup (240 mL) quick-cook
    rolled oats (not regular
    or instant)
1 ½ cups (360 mL) granola
1 cup (240 mL) raisins
1 ¼ cups (300 mL) chocolate
    chips
1 ¼ cups (300 mL) walnuts

Who could resist making something called Gorilla Cookies? This recipe was given to me by my friend Alan Miceli, who, as well as being a classical guitarist, Transcendental Meditation teacher and great guy, is an incredible baker. He sends me recipes from Vancouver, and when I mentioned I was doing a cookbook, he told me about Gorilla Cookies. They sounded delicious, but when I asked him why they were called Gorilla Cookies, he laughed and said: "No, no! Granola, not Gorilla!" Alan, I hope you don't mind, but I think "Gorilla" is a much better name and I'm afraid it stuck.

Preheat the oven to 350°F (175°C). Line two 18 x 12-inch (45 x 30-cm) baking sheets with parchment paper.

Using an electric mixer or a wooden spoon, cream the butter and sugar until light. Beat in the eggs one at a time, along with the vanilla. Combine the flour, baking soda, baking powder, salt and oats in a separate bowl. Add to the butter mixture and beat thoroughly. Fold in the granola, raisins, chocolate chips and walnuts. The mixture will be very stiff. Using a 1 ¼-inch (3-cm) ice cream scoop or a tablespoon, drop the cookie dough 3 inches (7.5 cm) apart on the prepared pans. Press slightly; the mixture will spread.

Bake for about 12 to 15 minutes, or until set but still soft. Cool for at least 2 minutes before removing to a wire rack to cool completely. Store in a tightly closed container for up to 5 days.

Triple Chocolate Chunk Cookies

Makes 2 dozen 2-inch (5-cm) cookies

1 cup (240 mL) butter,
softened

1 cup (240 mL) brown sugar

½ cup (120 mL) granulated
sugar

2 eggs

2 tsp. (10 mL) vanilla extract

2½ cups (600 mL) all-purpose
flour

1 tsp. (5 mL) baking soda

¼ tsp. (1.2 mL) salt

¾ cup (180 mL) semisweet
chocolate chunks

¾ cup (180 mL) milk
chocolate chunks

¾ cup (180 mL) white
chocolate chunks

1 cup (240 mL) macadamia nuts

If you love chocolate but can't decide which type is your favorite, then these cookies are for you. White, milk and semisweet chocolate chunks and macadamia nuts are barely contained in a buttery dough. This is a chocolate chip cookie all grown up.

Preheat the oven to 350°F (175°C). Line two 18 x 12-inch (45 x 30-cm) baking sheets with parchment paper.

Using an electric mixer, beat the butter and sugars until light and fluffy. Beat in the eggs and vanilla. Combine the flour, baking soda and salt in a separate bowl. Stir into the butter mixture. Stir in the chocolate chunks and nuts. Using a 1¼-inch (3-cm) ice cream scoop or tablespoon, drop the dough 2 inches (5 cm) apart on the prepared baking sheets.

Bake for 12 to 15 minutes, or until the cookies are slightly raised in the center and browned on the edges. Cool for at least 2 minutes before removing from the pans to a wire rack to cool completely. Store in a tightly closed container for up to 4 days.

Chocolate Raspberry Silk Tarte, page 84

Lemon Meringue Pie,
page 86

Citrus Lace Cups,
page 88

Chocolate Almond Kisses,
page 99

Choc–o–rama Cookies

Makes 2 dozen 2-inch (5-cm) cookies

¼ cup (60 mL) butter

8 oz. (225 g) semisweet chocolate, coarsely chopped

⅔ cup (160 mL) brown sugar

2 eggs

1 tsp. (5 mL) vanilla extract

½ cup (120 mL) all-purpose flour

1 tsp. (5 mL) baking powder

¼ tsp. (1.2 mL) salt

1¼ cups (300 mL) pecans

8 oz. (225 g) semisweet chocolate, broken into chunks

Chocolate, chocolate and more chocolate! Just how much chocolate is it possible to cram into a cookie? I suppose there are limits, and in this recipe be prepared to test them. These cookies are indulgent, I agree, but they are meant to be.

Preheat the oven to 325°F (165°C). Line two 18 x 12-inch (45 x 30-cm) baking sheets with parchment paper.

Melt the butter and coarsely chopped chocolate in a medium saucepan over low heat or in the microwave, stirring until smooth. Add the sugar, eggs and vanilla; stir until well mixed. Combine the flour, baking powder and salt in a separate bowl. Add to the chocolate mixture, stirring until well combined. Stir in the pecans and chocolate pieces, combining thoroughly. Using a 1¼-inch (3-cm) ice cream scoop or a tablespoon drop the cookie dough 2 inches (5 cm) apart on the prepared pans.

Bake for 15 to 17 minutes. Cool for 10 minutes on the pans before removing to a rack to cool completely. Store in a tightly closed container for up to 4 days.

Chocolate Lace Cookies

Makes 4 dozen 2-inch (5-cm) cookies

½ cup (120 mL) butter
1 cup (240 mL) brown sugar
½ cup (120 mL) corn syrup
1 cup (240 mL) almonds,
　finely chopped
1 cup (240 mL) pastry flour
1 tsp. (5 mL) vanilla extract
8 oz. (225 g) semisweet
　chocolate, coarsely chopped

These thin and crispy chocolate-covered cookies are impossible to resist. Brown sugar, nuts and butter always weaken my will-power—add chocolate and I'm in heaven.

Preheat the oven to 325°F (165°C). Line three 18 x 12-inch (45 x 30-cm) baking sheets with parchment paper.

Combine the butter, sugar and syrup in a medium saucepan and bring to a boil. Cook over medium heat for 1 minute, stirring occasionally. Remove from the heat and add the almonds, flour and vanilla, stirring until well mixed. Drop by teaspoonfuls 3 to 4 inches (7.5 to 10 cm) apart on the prepared sheets. Bake for 10 to 12 minutes, or until golden brown (check after about 8 minutes). Let cool on the pans, before removing carefully.

Melt the chocolate in a double boiler over hot water or in the microwave. Spread the melted chocolate on one side of each cookie and mark into ridges with a fork before the chocolate hardens. Store in a tightly closed container, with waxed paper between the layers, for up to 2 weeks.

Chocolate Almond Kisses

Makes 3 dozen 1½-inch (3.8-cm) cookies

8 oz. (225 g) semisweet chocolate, coarsely chopped

2 Tbsp. (30 mL) butter

1¼ cups (300 mL) almonds, finely ground

2 eggs

¾ cup (180 mL) granulated sugar

1 tsp. (5 mL) vanilla extract

¼ tsp. (1.2 mL) almond extract

½ cup (120 mL) icing sugar, sifted

These wonderfully chewy, gorgeous little morsels are loaded with chocolate and finely ground almonds, giving them the texture and flavor of chocolate marzipan.

Melt the chocolate and butter in the microwave or a double boiler, stirring until smooth. Add the almonds and stir until combined. In a separate bowl, and using an electric mixer or whisk, beat the eggs, sugar, vanilla, and almond extract until light and fluffy. Add the chocolate mixture and fold in thoroughly. Chill for at least 1 hour.

Preheat the oven to 350°F (175°C). Line two 18 x 12-inch (45 x 30-cm) baking sheets with parchment paper.

Form the dough into 1-inch (2.5-cm) balls and roll them in icing sugar. Place 2 inches (5 cm) apart on the prepared pans. Work quickly so the dough remains cold.

Bake for 10 to 12 minutes. The cookies will puff slightly and the surface will crack. Cool on the pans. Store in a tightly closed container for up to 1 week.

Coconut Almond Macaroons

Makes 3 dozen 2-inch (5-cm) cookies

2 cups (475 mL) icing sugar

2 cups (475 mL) shredded
sweetened coconut

2 1/3 cups (560 mL) almonds,
finely ground

1/2 tsp. (2.5 mL) almond
extract

1 Tbsp. (15 mL) lemon zest

5 egg whites, room temperature

6 oz. (180 g) semisweet chocolate, coarsely chopped

1 tsp. (5 mL) coconut oil or
vegetable shortening

The addition of ground almonds, lemon zest and almond extract gives a delicate taste and texture to these coconut macaroons. With or without the chocolate coating, they are irresistible.

Preheat the oven to 325°F (165°C). Line two 18 x 12-inch (45 x 30-cm) baking sheets with parchment paper.

Combine the icing sugar, coconut, almonds, almond extract and lemon zest. Using an electric mixer, beat the egg whites until stiff peaks form. Fold into the sugar mixture and combine gently but thoroughly. Using a 1 1/4-inch (3-cm) ice cream scoop, drop the cookie dough on the prepared cookie sheets about 2 inches (5 cm) apart.

Bake for 20 minutes or until golden. Cool completely on the pan.

Melt the chocolate and oil or shortening in a double boiler over hot water or in the microwave. Dip the cookies halfway into the chocolate. Place on parchment-lined cookie sheets and chill until the chocolate sets. Store in a tightly closed container for up to 1 week.

Hazelnut Macaroons

Makes 3 dozen 2-inch (5-cm) cookies

2 cups (475 mL) icing sugar

4¼ cups (1 L) blanched
   hazelnuts, finely ground

5 egg whites

1 tsp. (5 mL) vanilla extract

1½ Tbsp. (22.5 mL) hazelnut
   liqueur (optional)

8 oz. (225 g) milk chocolate,
   coarsely chopped

2 oz. (60 g) semisweet or
   white chocolate, coarsely
   chopped

Hazelnut and chocolate were made for each other. These moist chewy cookies keep very well if they are completely coated in chocolate. Wrapped in a festive box they make an elegant and very welcome gift.

Preheat the oven to 325°F (165°C). Line two 18 x 12-inch (45 x 30-cm) baking sheets with parchment paper.

Combine the icing sugar and hazelnuts. Using an electric mixer, beat the egg whites until stiff peaks form. Stir in the vanilla and liqueur, if desired. Fold in the icing sugar and hazelnut mixture, combining thoroughly. Using a 1¼-inch (3-cm) ice cream scoop, an oval shape if possible, drop the cookie dough on the prepared baking sheets about 2 inches (5 cm) apart.

Bake for 15 minutes. Cool completely on the pan.

Melt the milk chocolate in a double boiler over hot water or in the microwave, stirring occasionally. Dip the entire cookie in the melted chocolate. Place on parchment-lined cookie sheets and chill until the chocolate sets. Melt the semisweet or white chocolate in a small saucepan over low heat or in the microwave, stirring occasionally. Using a fork, decorate the top of the cookies with a chocolate squiggle. Store in a tightly closed container for up to 2 weeks.

Apricot Walnut Meringues

Makes 3½ dozen 2-inch (5-cm) cookies

½ cup (120 mL) egg whites

2 cups (475 mL) icing sugar

½ cup (120 mL) all-purpose flour

½ tsp. (2.5 mL) baking powder

1 tsp. (5 mL) vanilla extract

⅛ tsp. (.6 mL) salt

2 cups (475 mL) walnuts, coarsely chopped

⅔ cup (160 mL) dried apricots, coarsely chopped

This is a recipe that at first glance may not seem particularly appealing, but believe me, you will be sold on the first bite. The sweet crumble of meringue, the tart chewiness of apricots and the slightly bitter taste of walnuts all come together to create a unique and delectable cookie.

Preheat the oven to 325°F (165°C). Line two 18 x 12-inch (45 x 30-cm) baking sheets with parchment paper.

In a medium bowl, whisk the egg whites until frothy. Stir in the icing sugar, flour, baking powder, vanilla and salt. Add the walnuts and apricots and mix thoroughly. Using a 1¼-inch (3-cm) ice cream scoop or a tablespoon, drop the dough 2 inches (5 cm) apart onto the cookie sheets.

Bake for 15 to 18 minutes. Cool completely before removing from the pans. Store in a tightly closed container for up to 2 weeks.

Lemon Coconut Crisps

Makes 2 dozen 2-inch (5-cm) cookies

½ cup (120 mL) butter, softened

⅓ cup (80 mL) vegetable shortening

¾ cup (180 mL) granulated sugar

1 egg

1 tsp. (5 mL) vanilla extract

1½ Tbsp. (22.5 mL) grated lemon zest

2 cups (475 mL) pastry flour

½ tsp. (2.5 mL) salt

1 tsp. (5 mL) cream of tartar

½ tsp. (2.5 mL) baking soda

½ cup (120 mL) fine-shred sweetened coconut

This recipe comes to me "From the kitchen of Mary Cox." I still have the original recipe card for this delicious cookie given to me over 20 years ago. I never actually met Mary, but her daughter, Merredy, was kind enough to get the recipe for me after I tasted one of these tender lemon cookies. The recipe is perfect; don't even think of changing the shortening to butter, it is what gives these cookies their melt-in-your mouth texture. I have, however, successfully substituted 2 tsp. (10 mL) of baking powder for the cream of tartar and baking soda. Be sure to bake these cookies to a golden crispness, they are at their best that way. I love them with tea, but they are just as happy eaten any which way; they're not fussy.

Preheat the oven to 350°F (175°C). Line two 18 x 12-inch (45 x 30-cm) baking sheets with parchment paper.

Using an electric mixer or wooden spoon, cream the butter, shortening and sugar until light. Beat in the egg along with the vanilla and lemon zest. Combine the flour, salt, cream of tartar, baking soda and coconut in a separate bowl. Add to the butter mixture and beat thoroughly. Using a 1¼-inch (3-cm) ice cream scoop or tablespoon, drop the cookie dough on the prepared sheets. Press flat using a wide spatula lightly dusted with flour to prevent sticking.

Bake for 14 to 18 minutes, or until golden and slightly brown on the edges. Cool for at least 2 minutes on the pans before removing to a rack to cool completely. Store in a tightly closed container for up to 1 week.

Cinnamon Pecan Rugelach

Makes 32 2-inch (5-cm) cookies

FOR THE DOUGH:

2 ¼ cups (535 mL) all-purpose
flour

2 Tbsp. (30 mL) granulated
sugar

¼ tsp. (1.2 mL) salt

1 cup (240 mL) cold butter,
cut into chunks

1 cup (240 mL) cold cream
cheese, cut into chunks

2 Tbsp. (30 mL) sour cream

FOR THE FILLING:

1 cup (240 mL) pecans, finely
chopped

1 cup (240 mL) pecans,
coarsely chopped

¾ cup (180 mL) raisins

½ cup (120 mL) granulated
sugar

¼ cup (60 mL) brown sugar

1 tsp. (5 mL) ground
cinnamon

¾ cup (180 mL) raspberry
jam

If you have never had the pleasure of meeting one of these oh-so-tender, crumbly, jam-filled gems, then let me introduce you. Or if you have had the pleasure but it wasn't much of one, it's time to get reacquainted. When they are made right (that means no skipping on the cream cheese and other fattening stuff!), your guests will devour one right after the other, all the time exclaiming that they are just too rich. Make these goodies tiny, they are easier to eat and they bake up all the more crunchy.

FOR THE DOUGH: Combine the flour, sugar, salt, butter, cream cheese and sour cream in a food processor. Process, using short pulses, until the mixture resembles coarse meal. Continue mixing in short pulses until the dough just begins to come away from the sides of the bowl. Turn out onto a floured work surface and divide into 4 even pieces. Press into rounds, wrap in plastic and refrigerate for 2 hours.

Let sit at room temperature for 15 minutes before rolling. Roll into four 10-inch (2-cm) circles. Stack the circles, placing plastic wrap between them, and refrigerate or freeze.

FOR THE FILLING: Line two 18 x 12-inch (45 x 30-cm) baking sheets with parchment paper. Combine the pecans, raisins, sugars and cinnamon. Remove one circle of dough from the refrigerator (or freezer) at a time. Spread ¼ of the jam on each and sprinkle with ¼ of the nut mixture. Cut each circle into 8 wedges. Roll each wedge into the center of the circle to form a cylinder and then form into a crescent shape. Place 2 inches (5 cm) apart on the prepared baking sheets. Refrigerate for 20 to 30 minutes.

FOR THE TOPPING:

2 egg yolks

2 Tbsp. (30 mL) water

¼ cup (60 mL) granulated
   sugar

FOR THE TOPPING: Preheat the oven to 350°F (175°C). Whisk together the egg yolks and water and brush the tops of the crescents. Sprinkle with the sugar.

Bake for 20 to 25 minutes, until golden brown. Immediately after baking, carefully remove the cookies from the pan to a clean parchment lined cookie sheet. Cool. Store in a tightly closed container for up to 2 weeks.

VARIATION

CHOCOLATE APRICOT RUGELACH: Replace the raisins with chocolate chips and the raspberry jam with apricot jam.

Nut Crescents

⅞ cup (210 mL) butter,
  softened

¼ cup (60 mL) granulated
  sugar

2 egg yolks

1 tsp. (5 mL) vanilla extract

2 cups (475 mL) all-purpose
  flour

¼ tsp. (1.2 mL) salt

½ cup (120 mL) blanched
  almonds, finely ground

½ cup (120 mL) blanched
  hazelnuts, finely ground

⅓ cup (80 mL) granulated
  sugar

¼ cup (60 mL) icing sugar

Deceptively rich, these heavenly little tidbits simply melt in your mouth. Perfect with tea, perfect with milk, perfect any time.

Using an electric mixer or a wooden spoon, cream the butter and the ¼ cup (60 mL) granulated sugar. Add the egg yolks and vanilla and beat until light. In a separate bowl, combine the flour, salt and nuts. Stir into the butter mixture, mixing thoroughly. Cover and chill for 30 minutes.

Preheat the oven to 350°F (175°C). Line two 18 x 12-inch (45 x 30-cm) baking sheets with parchment paper.

Scoop walnut-sized balls of chilled dough and roll into ½-inch-thick (1.2-cm) ropes. Cut into 2-inch (5-cm) segments. Place on the prepared baking sheets and curve to form crescents. Bake for 12 minutes, or until golden.

Combine the remaining ⅓ cup (80 mL) granulated sugar and the icing sugar in a bowl. Toss the warm cookies gently in the mixture. Cool on a rack. Store in an airtight container for up to 2 weeks.

Bars and Squares

Quite often, a desperate urge for something rich, gooey and sweet can best be fulfilled by the sticky goodness of a bar or square. There is nothing quite like a buttery morsel, oozing caramel and chocolate and crunchy with toasted nuts, to satisfy that craving. This chapter is bursting with an array of tempting and delicious bars and squares, from simple lunchbox treats to light airy confections and bars so seductive and chocolatey that they are more candy than cookie.

Squares are perfect to whip up when you absolutely can't wait to satisfy that sweet tooth; most of these recipes come together quickly and effortlessly, and the delicious results belie the ease of their preparation. Sleek and sophisticated or casual and everyday, these recipes are sure to become part of your repertoire, as they are of mine.

Butterscotch Brownies

Makes 32 brownies

FOR THE BASE:

1 cup (240 mL) butter

2½ cups (600 mL) dark brown sugar

3 eggs

2 tsp. (10 mL) vanilla extract

1½ cups (360 mL) all-purpose flour

½ tsp. (2.5 mL) salt

1 Tbsp.(15 mL) baking powder

2 cups (475 mL) walnuts or pecans

FOR THE TOPPING:

1½ cups (360 mL) brown sugar

½ cup (120 mL) water

½ cup (120 mL) whipping cream

¼ cup (60 mL) butter, melted

1 tsp. (5 mL) vanilla extract

1 cup (240 mL) walnuts or pecans, coarsely chopped

There is no known cure! I know, because I spent one entire weekend baking these until the wee hours. We were participating in a food festival, where we featured this square. By the first evening we had sold out the whole weekend's allotment and I had to go back to the bakery to bake more for the next morning. We even put the price up in hopes of slowing down the frenzied consumption of our treat, but to no avail; the following evening I was back at the bakery, desperately baking for the next morning. You have been warned! There is no known cure!

FOR THE BASE: Preheat the oven to 325°F (165°C). Butter a 9 x 13-inch (23 x 33-cm) baking pan, line it with foil, and butter again. (Preparing the pan this way ensures a perfectly baked brownie that is easy to remove.)

Melt the butter in a small saucepan. Cool slightly. Using an electric mixer, cream the sugar, eggs and vanilla until light, about 4 minutes. Add the melted butter and mix thoroughly. In a separate bowl, combine the flour, salt and baking powder. Add to the egg mixture and mix well. Stir in the walnuts or pecans and spread in the pan. Bake for 40 to 45 minutes, until puffed in the center and golden. Do not overbake. Cool in the pan and then remove. Peel off the foil and place the brownie slab back into the pan.

FOR THE TOPPING: Bring the sugar and water to a boil in a small, heavy saucepan. Swirl the pan to ensure even caramelization. Cook without stirring to a medium golden color. Remove from the heat. Stirring carefully, add the cream slowly; be careful—the mixture will foam. Add the butter and vanilla. Cool until the mixture thickens but can still be poured. Spread over the cooled brownies and sprinkle with the nuts. Let the caramel set before cutting into 32 bars. Store in a tightly closed container for up to 5 days.

Cheesecake Brownies

Makes 32 brownies

FOR THE BASE:

8 oz. (225 g) semisweet chocolate, coarsely chopped

3 oz. (90 g) unsweetened chocolate, coarsely chopped

¾ cup (180 mL) butter

¼ cup (60 mL) cocoa

4 large eggs, room temperature

1¾ cups + 2 Tbsp. (450 mL) granulated sugar

2 tsp. (10 mL) vanilla extract

½ tsp. (2.5 mL) salt

1½ cups (360 mL) all-purpose flour

1½ tsp. (7.5 mL) baking powder

FOR THE TOPPING:

8 oz. (225 g) cream cheese, softened

2 Tbsp. (30 mL) butter, softened

½ cup (120 mL) granulated sugar

2 tsp. (10 mL) all-purpose flour

1 egg yolk

2 Tbsp. (30 mL) whipping cream

½ tsp. (2.5 mL) almond extract

FOR THE GLAZE (OPTIONAL):

1 oz. (30 g) each semisweet and white chocolate, coarsely chopped

Chewy and intensely chocolate, these brownies have a moist creamy texture and a surprisingly delicate flavor. With the addition of a swirl of velvety cream cheese, they are a sophisticated, bittersweet version of an old-fashioned classic.

FOR THE BASE: Preheat the oven to 325°F (165°C). Butter a 9 x 13-inch (23 x 33-cm) pan, line it with foil and butter again. (Preparing the pan this way ensures a perfectly baked brownie that is easy to remove.) Melt the chocolate and butter in a medium saucepan or in the microwave, stirring every minute until smooth. Add the cocoa and whisk until smooth. Using an electric mixer, beat the eggs, sugar, vanilla and salt on low speed for about 1 minute. Stir in the chocolate. Mix the flour and baking powder together, add them to the batter and mix until smooth. Spread into the prepared pan.

FOR THE TOPPING: Using an electric mixer or wooden spoon beat the cream cheese, butter and sugar until smooth. Stir in the flour, egg yolk, cream and almond extract and beat until well combined. Drop the mixture by tablespoons onto the brownie batter in the pan. Swirl gently. Bake for 45 minutes, or until barely set. Do not overbake. Cool for at least 2 hours before removing the foil. Cut into 32 bars. Store in a tightly closed container for up to 5 days.

FOR THE GLAZE (OPTIONAL): For a more elegant presentation, melt 1 oz. (30 g) dark and 1 oz. (30 g) white chocolate in double boilers over hot water or in the microwave. Drizzle alternately over the cooled brownies. Allow the chocolate to set before cutting into bars or squares.

Skor Brownies

Makes 32 brownies

FOR THE BASE:

1⅓ cups (320 mL) butter

4 eggs

1¼ cups (300 mL) granulated sugar

1¼ cups (300 mL) brown sugar

¼ cup (60 mL) very strong coffee, cooled

1 tsp. (5 mL) vanilla extract

1¼ cups (300 mL) high-quality Dutch cocoa

1 cup (240 mL) all-purpose flour

1½ tsp. (7.5 mL) baking powder

½ tsp. (2.5 mL) salt

1 cup (240 mL) pecans, coarsely chopped

FOR THE GANACHE TOPPING:

¼ cup (60 mL) butter

8 oz. (225 g) semisweet chocolate, coarsely chopped

½ cup (120 mL) whipping cream

2 Tbsp. (30 mL) corn syrup

1½ cups (360 mL) coarsely broken Skor bars

When I first introduced this brownie to our line-up of bars and squares, I had no idea how popular it would become. Dark chocolate ganache, gooey caramel and, of course, lots of broken Skor candy bars is an irresistible combination. When the Village Post *magazine picked the top 10 brownies in Toronto in April 2001, guess which brownie was the grand champion?*

FOR THE BASE: Preheat the oven to 350°F (175°C). Butter a 9 x 13-inch (23 x 33-cm) baking pan, line it with foil and butter again. (Preparing the pan this way ensures a perfectly baked brownie that is easy to remove.)

Melt the butter in a small saucepan over low heat or in the microwave. Using an electric mixer, beat the eggs, sugars, coffee and vanilla until light and fluffy, about 4 minutes. Add the melted butter and stir to combine. Combine the cocoa, flour, baking powder and salt in a separate bowl. Add to the beaten egg mixture, mixing well. Stir in the nuts. Spread the batter evenly in the prepared pan. Bake for 45 to 50 minutes, until slightly puffed in the center. Cool in the pan. Remove from the pan, peel off the foil and place the brownie slab back in the pan.

FOR THE GANACHE TOPPING: Melt the butter and chocolate in a medium saucepan over low heat or in a microwave, stirring occasionally. Stir in the cream and syrup. Spread on the cooled base. Distribute the Skor pieces evenly over the top, standing the pieces up if possible.

FOR THE CARAMEL:

1 ½ cups (360 mL) granulated
    sugar

½ cup (120 mL) water

2 Tbsp. (30 mL) corn syrup

½ cup (120 mL) whipping
    cream

¼ cup (60 mL) cold butter,
    cut into ½-inch (1.2-cm)
    pieces

1 tsp. (5 mL) vanilla extract

FOR THE CARAMEL: Bring the sugar, water and syrup to a boil in a heavy saucepan over medium heat, stirring constantly. When the mixture begins to boil, reduce the heat to medium-low and cook without stirring to a medium golden color. Remove from the heat. Stirring carefully, slowly pour in the cream. Add the butter and vanilla and stir to combine. Cool slightly and then drizzle over the brownies. Let the caramel set before cutting into bars or squares. Store in a tightly closed container for up to 5 days.

White Chocolate Brownies

Makes 32 brownies

FOR THE BASE:

1 cup (240 mL) butter

1 lb. (455 g) white chocolate, coarsely chopped

4 eggs, room temperature

1 cup (240 mL) granulated sugar

2 tsp. (10 mL) vanilla extract

2 cups (475 mL) all-purpose flour

1 tsp. (5 mL) baking powder

$\frac{1}{2}$ tsp. (2.5 mL) salt

8 oz. (225 g) semisweet or bittersweet chocolate, coarsely chopped

1 cup (240 mL) diced almonds, lightly toasted

FOR THE TOPPING:

2 oz. (57 g) white chocolate, coarsely chopped

2 oz. (57 g) bittersweet or semisweet chocolate, coarsely chopped

White chocolate is the star of this brownie, providing a delicate sweetness and creamy, soft texture that is perfectly balanced by the bittersweet chocolate chunks and crunchy toasted almonds. A very grown-up brownie.

FOR THE BASE: Preheat the oven to 325°F (165°C). Butter a 9 x 13-inch (23 x 33-cm) baking pan, line with foil and butter again. (Preparing the pan this way ensures a perfectly baked brownie that is easy to remove.)

Melt the butter in a medium saucepan over low heat or in the microwave. When it is hot and bubbly, add half the white chocolate, stir once and set aside.

Using an electric mixer, beat the eggs, sugar and vanilla until light and fluffy. Stir the melted white chocolate until smooth. Add it to the egg mixture and beat until smooth.

Combine the flour, baking powder and salt in a separate bowl. Add to the chocolate mixture. Mix until well blended. Stir in the remaining white chocolate, dark chocolate and almonds. Spread the batter in the prepared pan. Bake for 40 to 45 minutes, until puffed in the center and starting to turn golden. Cool in the pan for at least 4 to 6 hours before removing. Peel off the foil and place the brownie slab back in the pan.

FOR THE TOPPING: Melt the white chocolate and dark chocolate separately in double boilers over hot water or in the microwave. Drizzle over the cooled brownies. Allow the chocolate to set before cutting into bars or squares. Store in a tightly closed container for up to 5 days.

Rocky Road Brownies

Makes 32 brownies

FOR THE BASE:

1⅓ cups (320 mL) butter

4 eggs

1¼ cups (300 mL) granulated sugar

1¼ cups (300 mL) brown sugar

1 tsp. (5 mL) vanilla extract

1¼ cups (300 mL) high-quality Dutch cocoa

1 cup (240 mL) all-purpose flour

1½ tsp. (7.5 mL) baking powder

½ tsp. (2.5 mL) salt

FOR THE TOPPING:

1 cup (240 mL) milk

⅓ cup (80 mL) high-quality Dutch cocoa

1 cup (240 mL) granulated sugar

½ cup (120 mL) butter

⅓ cup (80 mL) corn syrup

pinch of salt

5 oz. (140 g) semisweet chocolate, finely chopped

1 tsp. (5 mL) vanilla extract

20 large marshmallows cut in quarters

1 cup (240 mL) broken pecans or peanuts

8 oz. (225 g) semisweet chocolate, coarsely chopped

Take marshmallows, toasted nuts and chocolate, melt and swirl them together on top of a dark fudgy brownie, and then stand back. No man, woman or child can resist this combination of gooey, sweet and crunchy.

FOR THE BASE: Preheat the oven to 350°F (175°C). Butter a 9 x 13-inch (23 x 33-cm) baking pan, line with foil and butter again. (Preparing the pan this way ensures a perfectly baked brownie that is easy to remove.)

Melt the butter in a small saucepan over low heat or in the microwave. Using an electric mixer, beat the eggs, sugars and vanilla until light and fluffy. Add the melted butter and stir to combine. In a separate bowl, mix the cocoa, flour, baking powder and salt. Add to the beaten egg mixture, stirring until well combined. Spread the batter evenly in the prepared pan. Bake for 45 to 50 minutes.

FOR THE TOPPING: While the brownies are baking, prepare the topping. In a heavy saucepan, combine the milk, cocoa, sugar, butter, corn syrup and salt. Cook over medium heat, stirring constantly, until the sugar is dissolved and the mixture begins to boil. Reduce the heat to low and simmer for 10 to 15 minutes without stirring. Remove from the heat. Add the 5 oz. (140 g) finely chopped chocolate and the vanilla, but do not stir. After 15 minutes, stir to combine.

When you remove the brownies from the oven, cover the hot brownies with the marshmallow quarters. Sprinkle with the pecans or peanuts and the 8 oz. (225 g) coarsely chopped chocolate. Return to the oven for 15 minutes. Remove from the oven and pour the chocolate sauce over top of the brownies and swirl with a knife. Cool in the pan for 4 to 5 hours and then remove. Peel off the foil and cut into bars or squares. Store in a tightly closed container for up to 5 days.

Butter Tart Squares

Makes 32 squares

FOR THE CRUST:

1 cup (240 mL) cold butter, cut into ½-inch (1.2-cm) pieces

2 cups (475 mL) all-purpose flour

3 Tbsp. (45 mL) granulated sugar

FOR THE FILLING:

1 cup (240 mL) raisins

1 cup (240 mL) hot water

4 eggs

2¼ cups (535 mL) brown sugar

⅓ cup (80 mL) corn syrup

2 tsp. (10 mL) vinegar

2 tsp. (10 mL) vanilla extract

2 Tbsp. (30 mL) all-purpose flour

½ cup (120 mL) butter, melted

1 cup (240 mL) pecans or walnuts, coarsely chopped

Big brother to the little butter tart, just as yummy but a lot faster to make. For those occasions when waiting is not an option.

FOR THE CRUST: Preheat the oven to 350°F (175°C). Using a food processor or pastry blender, process or cut the butter into the flour and sugar until the mixture is mealy. Mix until it is just starting to come together and no longer looks dry. Press onto the bottom and 1 inch (2.5 cm) up the sides of a 9 x 13-inch (23 x 33-cm) baking pan. Bake for about 15 minutes, until set and barely golden.

FOR THE FILLING: Soak the raisins in the hot water for 15 minutes. Drain. Combine the eggs, sugar, syrup, vinegar, vanilla and flour in a medium bowl. Whisk until smooth. Whisk in the butter. Stir in the soaked raisins and the nuts. Pour into the baked crust. Bake for 25 to 35 minutes, or until golden and no longer liquid in the center. Cool completely before cutting into bars or squares. Store in the refrigerator in a tightly closed container for up to 5 days.

Date Squares

Makes 32 squares

1 lb. (455 g) dates, roughly
chopped

1 cup (240 mL) water

½ cup (120 mL) granulated
sugar

¼ cup (60 mL) lemon juice

½ cup (120 mL) walnuts

1 cup (240 mL) butter, softened

1 cup (240 mL) brown sugar

1 tsp. (5 mL) vanilla extract

1 ½ cups (360 mL) all-purpose
flour

1 ½ cups (360 mL) quick-cook
rolled oats (not regular
or instant)

1 tsp. (5 mL) baking soda

½ tsp. (2.5 mL) salt

*Butter-crumbly outside, moist and fruity inside, this old standby
never fails to please. It's one of those unassuming squares that
doesn't seem worth bothering with—until you start eating it. Did
you know that they were originally known as matrimonial squares?*

In a medium saucepan, combine the dates, water and granulated
sugar. Simmer until soft, about 5 to 10 minutes, stirring
frequently. Remove from the heat. Stir in the lemon juice and
walnuts. Cool slightly.

Preheat the oven to 375°F (190°C). Butter a 9 x 13-inch
(23 x 33-cm) baking pan. Cream the butter with the brown
sugar and vanilla. Combine the flour, oats, baking soda and salt
in a separate bowl. Add to the butter/sugar mixture and stir
until just combined. Press a little more than half the mixture
into the prepared pan. Spread the date filling over the base.
Crumble the remaining mixture over the top. Bake for 25 to
30 minutes, or until the topping is golden. Cool completely
before cutting into squares. Store in a tightly covered container
for up to 1 week.

Apple Cream Cheese Squares

Makes 32 bars

FOR THE CRUST:

¾ cup (180 mL) cold butter, cut into ½-inch (1.2-cm) pieces

2 cups (475 mL) all-purpose flour

¼ cup (60 mL) icing sugar

3 Tbsp. (45 mL) water

FOR THE FILLING:

12 oz. (340 g) cream cheese, room temperature

⅓ cup (80 mL) granulated sugar

1 egg

1 tsp. (5 mL) vanilla extract

½ tsp. (2.5 mL) almond extract

¼ tsp. (1.2 mL) salt

6 cups (1.5 L) apple slices cut ¼ inch (.6 cm) thick

⅓ cup (80 mL) granulated sugar

1 tsp. (5 mL) ground cinnamon

2 Tbsp. (30 mL) cornstarch

1 Tbsp. (15 mL) lemon juice

The different elements of this recipe combine in an almost magical fashion, making the end result much more than the sum of its parts. This became very apparent to me as I watched this square become increasingly popular with our customers, who are like disappointed children when we sell out of their favorite treat. "But I came all the way across town for one of these squares!" For a change, try cherries instead of apples; in my opinion, it is even more scrumptious, but cherries are always my number one choice.

FOR THE CRUST: Preheat the oven to 350°F (175°C). Line a 9 x 13-inch (23 x 33-cm) baking pan with 2 overlapping pieces of parchment paper that extend up the sides and over the top of the pan by 1 inch (2.5 cm). The extra paper on all sides of the pan makes it easy to lift the finished slab out of the pan without having to flip it over.

Using a food processor or a pastry blender, process or cut the butter into the flour and icing sugar until the mixture is mealy. Add the water and continue mixing until the dough is just starting to come together in a ball. Press into the bottom and ½ inch (1.2 cm) up the sides of the prepared pan. Bake for about 15 minutes, until set and slightly golden.

FOR THE FILLING: Using an electric mixer or a wooden spoon, beat the cream cheese and sugar until smooth. Add the egg, vanilla, almond extract and salt and combine thoroughly. Spread in the prepared crust. Combine the apples, sugar, cinnamon, cornstarch and lemon juice. Spread over the cream cheese layer.

FOR THE TOPPING:

¾ cup (180 mL) cold butter, cut into ½-inch (1.2-cm) pieces

1 ½ cups (360 mL) all-purpose flour

1 ½ cups (360 mL) granulated sugar

1 cup (240 mL) sliced almonds

FOR THE TOPPING: Using a food processor or pastry cutter, process or cut the butter into the flour and sugar until the dough is just beginning to clump. Spread over the apples. Sprinkle with the almonds.

Bake for 45 to 55 minutes, until the topping is golden and the apples are tender. Cool completely before cutting into bars or squares. Store in the refrigerator in a tightly closed container for up to 5 days.

VARIATION

CHERRY CREAM CHEESE SQUARES: Omit the lemon juice and cinnamon and substitute 6 cups (1.5 L) of pitted sour cherries for the apples.

Lemon Coconut Squares

Makes 32 squares

FOR THE CRUST:

1 cup cold butter, cut into
  $\frac{1}{2}$-inch (1.2-cm) pieces
2 cups (475 mL) all-purpose
  flour
3 Tbsp. (45 mL) granulated
  sugar

FOR THE FILLING:

8 eggs
2 $\frac{1}{2}$ cups (600 mL) granulated
  sugar
1 tsp. (5 mL) vanilla extract
1 Tbsp. (15 mL) lemon zest
$\frac{1}{2}$ cup (120 mL) all-purpose
  flour
2 tsp. (10 mL) baking powder
3 cups (720 mL) sweetened
  flaked coconut
1 $\frac{1}{4}$ cups (300 mL) freshly
  squeezed lemon juice
icing sugar, for dusting

This tangy treat has quickly become one of our bestsellers, rivaled only by our Skor Brownie (page 110). The buttery short-bread crust is a perfect base for the silky lemon filling, and the sweetened coconut floats to the top during baking, forming a tender crust. Irresistible.

FOR THE CRUST: Preheat the oven to 350°F (175°C). Using a food processor or pastry blender, process or cut the butter into the flour and sugar until it is just starting to come together and no longer looks dry. Press into the bottom and $\frac{1}{2}$ inch (1.2 cm) up the sides of a 9 x 13-inch (23 x 33-cm) baking pan. Bake for about 15 minutes, until set and barely golden.

FOR THE FILLING: Using an electric mixer or whisk, beat the eggs and sugar until very light and thick, about 5 minutes. Beat in the vanilla and lemon zest. In a separate bowl combine the flour, baking powder and coconut. Stir into the egg mixture and then stir in the lemon juice. Pour into the baked crust. Return to the oven and bake until set, about 30 minutes. Cool completely in the pan before cutting into squares. Store in a tightly closed container for up to 5 days. Dust lightly with icing sugar before serving.

Orange Pecan Squares

Makes 32 squares

FOR THE CRUST:

¾ cup (180 mL) cold butter, cut into ½-inch (1.2-cm) pieces

2 cups (475 mL) all-purpose flour

¼ cup (60 mL) icing sugar

3 Tbsp. (45 mL) water

FOR THE FILLING:

3 eggs

2¼ cups (535 mL) brown sugar

2 tsp. (10 mL) vanilla extract

3 Tbsp. (45 mL) all-purpose flour

¾ tsp. (3.7 mL) baking powder

½ tsp. (2.5 mL) salt

1½ cups (360 mL) pecans, finely chopped

1 cup (240 mL) shredded coconut

FOR THE ICING:

1 cup (240 mL) butter, softened

2½ cups (600 mL) icing sugar

¼ cup (60 mL) Grand Marnier or other orange liqueur

2 tsp. (10 mL) orange zest

1 tsp. (5 mL) vanilla extract

1 Tbsp. (15 mL) lemon juice

This is another one of those recipes that I can't remember ever being without. The sweet chewy filling full of pecans, coconut and brown sugar is set off perfectly by the tender shortbread crust and buttery orange icing. Cut these squares into small pieces—they are very rich.

FOR THE CRUST: Preheat the oven to 350°F (175°C). Using a food processor or a pastry blender, cut the butter into the flour and icing sugar until the mixture is mealy. Add the water and continue mixing until the dough is just starting to come together in a ball. Press onto the bottom and ½ inch (1.2 cm) up the sides of a 9 x 13-inch (23 x 33-cm) baking pan. Bake for about 15 minutes, until set and slightly golden.

FOR THE FILLING: Using an electric mixer or whisk, beat the eggs slightly. Add the sugar and vanilla and beat until just blended. Combine the flour, baking powder, salt, pecans and coconut in a separate bowl. Add to the beaten eggs and mix until well combined. Pour into the baked crust. Bake for 25 to 30 minutes, until golden brown. Cool in the pan.

FOR THE ICING: Using an electric mixer, cream the butter until fluffy. Add the icing sugar gradually and beat until light. Add the liqueur, orange zest, vanilla and lemon juice. Beat until smooth and creamy. Spread over the cooled filling. Allow to set before cutting into squares. Store in a tightly closed container for up to 1 week.

Orange Almond Bars

Makes 12 bars

FOR THE BASE:

½ cup (120 mL) butter,
softened

½ cup (120 mL) granulated
sugar

1 tsp. (5 mL) vanilla extract

¼ tsp. (1.2 mL) salt

4 eggs, separated

⅓ cup (80 mL) freshly
squeezed orange juice

1 Tbsp. (15 mL) orange zest

3 Tbsp. (45 mL) granulated
sugar

⅔ cup (160 mL) all-purpose
flour

1 tsp. (5 mL) baking powder

1 cup (240 mL) ground
almonds

FOR THE ICING:

1¾ cups (420 mL) icing sugar

¼ cup (60 mL) orange juice

1 tsp. (5 mL) orange zest

1 Tbsp. (15 mL) Grand Marnier
or other orange liqueur

½ tsp. (2.5 mL) vanilla
extract

TO ASSEMBLE:

⅔ cup (160 mL) orange
marmalade

This elegant and delicate treat is the perfect dessert to serve at an afternoon tea or shower. Folding in beaten egg whites and baking the batter in a large baking sheet ensures an incredibly light and tender texture. If you love the flavor of oranges, this recipe will immediately become a favorite.

FOR THE BASE: Preheat the oven to 400°F (200°C). Butter a 9 x 13-inch (23 x 33-cm) pan and line it with parchment paper. Butter it again and then dust with flour.

Using an electric mixer, cream the butter, ½ cup (120 mL) sugar, vanilla and salt until light and fluffy. Beat in the egg yolks one at a time, beating for about 30 seconds after each addition. Stir in the juice and zest.

In a separate bowl, beat the egg whites with an electric mixer until soft peaks form. Add the 3 Tbsp. (45 mL) sugar and beat until stiff but still glossy. Fold the egg whites into the butter mixture.

Sift the flour and baking powder together and combine with the almonds. Gently fold the flour-nut mixture into the egg mixture. Spread in the prepared pan. Bake for 10 to 15 minutes, or until just set. Cool in the pan and then remove carefully.

FOR THE ICING: Combine the icing sugar, orange juice, zest, liqueur and vanilla. Whisk to pouring consistency.

TO ASSEMBLE: Cut the cooled base lengthwise into 2 even pieces. Using a food processor, purée the marmalade until smooth. Spread over one layer and cover with the second layer. Spread the icing over the top. Cut into bars when the icing sets. Store in a tightly closed container for up to 3 days.

Toffee Bars

Makes 32 bars

FOR THE CRUST:

1 cup (240 mL) butter,
    softened

1 cup (240 mL) brown sugar

2 egg yolks

1 tsp. (5 mL) vanilla extract

1 cup (240 mL) all-purpose
    flour

1 cup (240 mL) quick-cook
    rolled oats (not regular
    or instant)

½ tsp. (2.5 mL) salt

FOR THE TOPPING:

9 oz. (255 g) semisweet
    chocolate, coarsely chopped

3 Tbsp. (45 mL) butter

1 cup (240 mL) chopped
    pecans

At first glance this recipe seems to have far too much butter in proportion to the other ingredients. No chance of that—the richness of the crust is what makes this bar so impossibly tender and delicious. To make it even more enticing, the recipe is absolutely effortless. Just be sure to use the best quality chocolate.

FOR THE CRUST: Preheat the oven to 375°F (190°C). Butter a 9 x 13-inch (23 x 33-cm) baking pan. Cream the butter and sugar with a wooden spoon. Beat in the egg yolks and vanilla. Add the flour, oats and salt and combine to make a thick dough. Press into the prepared pan. Bake for 20 to 25 minutes, until golden brown. Cool slightly.

FOR THE TOPPING: Melt the chocolate and butter in a double boiler over hot water or in the microwave. Spread on the baked base. Sprinkle the pecans over top, pressing them slightly into the chocolate. Cool and cut into bars. Store in a tightly closed container for up to 1 week.

Peanut Butter Crunch

Makes 32 bars

FOR THE BASE:

¼ cup (60 mL) butter

1¼ cups (300 mL) brown sugar

1½ cups (360 mL) corn syrup

1¼ cups (300 mL) peanut butter

1 tsp. (5 mL) vanilla extract

4½ cups (1.1 mL) rice cereal

2½ cups (600 mL) peanuts

FOR THE TOPPING:

¼ cup (60 mL) butter

½ cup (120 mL) whipping cream

8 oz. (225 g) semisweet chocolate, coarsely chopped

2 Tbsp. (30 mL) corn syrup

Unabashedly sweet and gooey, these addictive squares don't even pretend to be anything other than what they are—candy. What else do you call sticky, chocolate-covered caramel, full of peanuts, rice cereal and peanut butter? They are ridiculously simple to prepare and dangerously easy to eat. Be sure to cut these squares into small pieces—a little goes a long way.

FOR THE BASE: Line a 9 x 13-inch (23 x 33-cm) pan with parchment paper and butter lightly.

Melt the butter in a very large saucepan over medium heat. Add the sugar and cook, stirring constantly, until the sugar dissolves completely. Add the corn syrup, peanut butter and vanilla, and continue cooking until the mixture is hot and smooth. Do not boil. Combine the rice cereal and peanuts and add to the saucepan. Stir to combine thoroughly. Spread the hot mixture in the prepared pan, pressing with your hands or with a rolling pin to flatten it. Cool completely before topping.

FOR THE TOPPING: In a medium saucepan over medium heat, heat the butter and cream until bubbly. Add the chocolate and allow to sit for 5 minutes. Stir until the chocolate is completely melted and then add the corn syrup. Cool until the mixture thickens slightly. Spread on the cooled base. Chill before cutting into bars or squares. Store in the refrigerator in a tightly closed container for up to 1 week.

With Coffee and Tea

With apologies to the pie gods, I confess that writing this chapter was as much fun as writing the one on fruit pies. Secretly, I will even admit it was actually more fun and I can't wait to do another cookbook, so I can include all the recipes I missed this time around. I guess coffee cakes, muffins, sticky buns, scones, bread puddings, tarts and quick breads each deserve their own chapter, but putting them all together in a big gooey mess is much more tantalizing!

Mocha Coffee Cake

Makes one 9-inch (23-cm) cake (serves 8 to 10)

FOR THE CAKE:

¾ cup (180 mL) butter, softened

1 cup (240 mL) granulated sugar

2 eggs

1 tsp. (5 mL) vanilla extract

2¼ cups (535 mL) all-purpose flour

1 tsp. (5 mL) baking powder

½ tsp. (2.5 mL) baking soda

½ tsp. (2.5 mL) salt

1¼ cups (300 mL) sour cream

1 Tbsp. (15 mL) instant coffee granules

2 tsp. (10 mL) hot water

¾ cup (180 mL) brown sugar

½ cup (120 mL) walnuts

2 Tbsp. (30 mL) melted butter

FOR THE TOPPING:

½ cup (120 mL) brown sugar

½ cup (120 mL) walnuts

FOR THE GLAZE:

¼ cup (60 mL) butter

½ cup (120 mL) granulated sugar

¼ cup (60 mL) whipping cream

½ tsp. (2.5 mL) vanilla extract

1½ tsp. (7.5 mL) instant coffee granules

2 oz. (57 g) semisweet chocolate, coarsely chopped

Don't let the tame appearance fool you, this is actually an indulgently rich dessert disguised as a simple coffee cake. Begin with sour cream batter, then swirl, sprinkle and drizzle with generous amounts of butter, chocolate, walnuts, brown sugar, coffee and heavy cream. Bake and drizzle some more, and then serve. Guaranteed to have your undivided attention after one bite.

FOR THE CAKE: Preheat the oven to 350°F (175°C). Butter and flour a 9-inch (23-cm) springform pan. Using an electric mixer, cream the butter and granulated sugar until light. Add the eggs and vanilla and beat until fluffy. In a separate bowl combine the flour, baking powder, baking soda and salt. Add the dry ingredients to the egg mixture in 3 parts, alternating with the sour cream. Mix well after each addition, scraping the bowl as necessary.

Dissolve the coffee in the hot water. Remove ⅓ of the batter to another bowl and add the coffee mixture. Combine the brown sugar, walnuts and melted butter. Spread half of the remaining batter in the prepared pan. Cover with the coffee-flavored batter and then the brown sugar-walnut mixture. Top with the remaining batter.

FOR THE TOPPING: Combine the sugar and walnuts and sprinkle over the batter in the pan. Bake for 50 to 60 minutes or until a cake tester inserted in the center comes out clean.

FOR THE GLAZE: Combine the butter, sugar, cream, vanilla and instant coffee in a small saucepan over medium heat or in a microwave. Bring to a simmer and cook until the sugar dissolves. Pour over the warm cake. Cool the cake completely before removing it from the pan. Melt the chocolate in a double boiler or in the microwave and drizzle over the cooled cake. Store in a tightly closed container at room temperature for up to 4 days.

Wild Blueberry Coffee Cake

Makes one 9-inch (23-cm) cake (serves 8 to 10)

FOR THE CAKE:

½ cup (120 mL) butter, softened

1¼ cups (300 mL) granulated sugar

2 eggs

1 tsp. (5 mL) vanilla extract

2¼ cups (535 mL) all-purpose flour

1 tsp. (5 mL) baking soda

¼ tsp. (1.2 mL) salt

1 cup (240 mL) sour cream

5½ cups (1.4 L) wild blueberries, approximately 1½ lb. (680 g), fresh or frozen

FOR THE TOPPING:

¾ cup (180 mL) brown sugar

½ cup (120 mL) broken walnuts

¼ tsp. (1.2 mL) ground cinnamon

FOR THE GLAZE:

¼ cup (60 mL) butter

½ cup (120 mL) granulated sugar

¼ cup (60 mL) whipping cream

½ tsp. (2.5 mL) vanilla extract

Although perfect for afternoon coffee break, the rich sour cream batter and wickedly indulgent glaze make this cake a tempting treat for any occasion.

FOR THE CAKE: Preheat the oven to 350°F (175°C). Butter and flour a 9-inch (23-cm) springform pan.

Using an electric mixer, cream the butter and sugar until light. Add the eggs and vanilla, and beat until fluffy. In a separate bowl, combine the flour, baking soda and salt. Add the dry ingredients to the egg mixture in 3 parts, alternating with the sour cream. Mix well after each addition, scraping the bowl as necessary. Fold in the blueberries and spread in the prepared pan.

FOR THE TOPPING: Combine the sugar, walnuts and cinnamon. Sprinkle over the batter in the pan. Bake for 50 to 60 minutes, or until a cake tester inserted in the center comes out clean.

FOR THE GLAZE: Combine the butter, sugar, cream and vanilla in a small saucepan over medium heat or in the microwave. Bring to a simmer and cook until the sugar dissolves. Pour over the warm cake. Cool the cake completely before removing it from the pan. Store refrigerated in a tightly covered container for up to 4 days.

VARIATIONS

RHUBARB COFFEE CAKE: Replace the blueberries with sliced rhubarb. Add ½ tsp. (2.5 mL) almond extract and 2 tsp. (10 mL) orange zest to the batter.

ORANGE CRANBERRY COFFEE CAKE: Replace the blueberries with cranberries. Add 1 tsp. (5 mL) orange zest to the batter, and use diced almonds instead of walnuts.

Almond Coffee Cake

Makes one 9-inch (23-cm) cake (serves 8 to 10)

FOR THE CAKE:

¾ cup (180 mL) butter, softened

1 cup (240 mL) granulated sugar

2 eggs

1 tsp. (5 mL) vanilla extract

1 tsp. (5 mL) almond extract

2¼ cups (535 mL) all-purpose flour

1 tsp. (5 mL) baking powder

½ tsp. (2.5 mL) baking soda

¼ tsp. (1.2 mL) salt

1¼ cups (300 mL) sour cream

¾ cup (180 mL) brown sugar

½ cup (120 mL) toasted sliced almonds

2 Tbsp. (30 mL) butter, melted

FOR THE TOPPING:

½ cup (120 mL) brown sugar

½ cup (120 mL) sliced almonds

FOR THE GLAZE:

¼ cup (60 mL) butter

½ cup (120 mL) granulated sugar

¼ cup (60 mL) whipping cream

1 tsp. (5 mL) vanilla extract

1 tsp. (5 mL) almond extract

I just couldn't resist including two almond coffee cakes in this chapter; this wonderfully moist and fragrant version, layered with buttery ground almonds and a sour cream batter, evolved from my original fruit coffee cake recipe. I adore almonds so much that I made sure to pack in as many as possible, resulting in an impossibly rich and delicious cake. Serve it slightly warm for afternoon tea and there won't be a crumb left.

FOR THE CAKE: Preheat the oven to 350°F (175°C). Butter and flour a 9-inch (23-cm) springform pan.

Using an electric mixer, cream the softened butter and granulated sugar until light. Add the eggs, vanilla and almond extract, and beat until fluffy. In a separate bowl combine the flour, baking powder, baking soda and salt. Add the dry ingredients to the egg mixture in 3 parts, alternating with the sour cream. Mix well after each addition, scraping the bowl as necessary. Combine the brown sugar, almonds and melted butter. Spread half the batter in the prepared pan. Sprinkle the brown sugar-almond mixture over the batter. Top with the remaining batter.

FOR THE TOPPING: Combine the brown sugar and almonds. Sprinkle over the top of the batter. Bake for 50 to 60 minutes, or until a cake tester inserted in the center comes out clean.

FOR THE GLAZE: Combine the butter, sugar, cream, vanilla and almond extract in a small saucepan over medium heat or in a microwave. Bring to a simmer and cook until the sugar dissolves. Pour over the warm cake. Cool the cake completely before removing it from the pan. Store at room temperature in a tightly closed container for up to 4 days.

Cinnamon Sour Cream Coffee Cake

Makes one 10-inch (25-cm) cake (serves 10 to 12)

1 cup (240 mL) butter,
softened

2 cups (475 mL) granulated
sugar

1 tsp. (5 mL) vanilla extract

3 eggs

1 ½ cups (360 mL) all-purpose
flour

1 cup (240 mL) pastry flour

½ tsp. (2.5 mL) salt

3 tsp. (15 mL) baking powder

1 ¼ tsp. (6 mL) baking soda

1 ½ cups (360 mL) sour cream

1 Tbsp. (15 mL) cocoa

1 Tbsp. (15 mL) ground
cinnamon

⅔ cup (160 mL) brown sugar

½ cup (120 mL) pecans or
walnuts

Simple, uncomplicated, but oh so rich and moist, this coffee cake can be assembled and in the oven in 15 minutes. What better way to get your sleepy weekend guests out of bed than with the delicious smell of warm cinnamon and toasted pecans?

Preheat the oven to 350°F (175°C). Butter and flour a 10-inch (25-cm) bundt pan.

Using an electric mixer, cream the butter and granulated sugar until light and fluffy. Add the vanilla and then the eggs, one at a time. Beat well after each addition. Combine both flours, salt, baking powder and baking soda in a separate bowl. Add the dry ingredients to the butter mixture in 3 parts, alternating with the sour cream. Mix well after each addition, scraping the bowl as necessary.

Combine the cocoa, cinnamon, brown sugar and nuts in a separate bowl. Stir until well mixed. Pour half the batter into the prepared pan. Sprinkle ⅓ of the cinnamon mixture over top. Add the remaining ½ of the batter and then the remaining ⅔ of the topping. Bake for 50 to 60 minutes, until a cake tester inserted in the center of the cake comes out clean. Cool for 15 minutes before inverting the pan and carefully removing the cake. Serve slightly warm. Store at room temperature in a tightly covered container for up to 3 days.

Raised Almond Coffee Cake

Makes two 9-inch (23-cm) cakes (each serves 8)

FOR THE DOUGH:

1 envelope active dry yeast
(2¼ tsp./11 mL)

4 Tbsp. (60 mL) granulated
sugar

2 Tbsp. (30 mL) warm water,
105° to 115°F (40° to 45°C)

½ tsp. (2.5 mL) salt

1 large egg, lightly beaten

½ cup (120 mL) light cream

2 cups (475 mL) all-purpose
flour, sifted

½ cup (120 mL) butter,
softened

FOR THE FILLING:

1 cup (240 mL) blanched
almonds

¾ cup (180 mL) granulated
sugar

½ cup (120 mL) fine breadcrumbs

2 Tbsp. (30 mL) butter,
melted

1 egg, beaten

½ tsp. (2.5 mL) almond
extract

1 tsp. (5 mL) vanilla extract

¼ cup (60 mL) butter, melted

Similar to classic Danish pastry, this tender, flaky coffee cake is a great way to try your hand at yeast baking. The key to preparing this type of pastry is the way the cool butter is layered, rolled and chilled. It is not difficult, as long as you allow for the proper amount of time required to chill the dough between turns. This recipe makes two cakes, one of which can be frozen unbaked and stored for several weeks. Just thaw it and allow it to rise before baking.

FOR THE DOUGH: Sprinkle the yeast and 1 Tbsp. (15 mL) of the sugar over the warm water in a medium bowl. Stir to dissolve. Let stand until foamy, about 5 minutes. Stir until smooth. Stir in the remaining 3 Tbsp. (45 mL) sugar, salt, egg and cream. Add 1½ cups (360 mL) of the flour and beat until smooth. Stir in the remaining flour to make a stiff dough. Turn out onto a floured work surface. Roll to ¼ inch (.6 cm) thickness. Spread the butter on the upper ⅔ of the dough and fold the lower ⅓ over the mid-dle ⅓. Fold the top ⅓ over that. Do a quarter-turn and roll again to ¼ inch (.6 cm) thickness. Fold in thirds. Cover and chill for 30 minutes. Repeat the rolling, folding and chilling three times.

FOR THE FILLING: Finely grind the almonds with ¼ cup (60 mL) of the sugar in a food processor. Add the remaining ½ cup (120 mL) sugar, breadcrumbs, 2 Tbsp. (30 mL) butter, egg, and almond and vanilla extracts. Mix thoroughly.

Divide the dough in half; roll each piece into a rectangle about 8 inches (20 cm) long and 6 inches (15 cm) wide. Brush the ¼ cup (60 mL) melted butter over each rectangle. Spread the filling over the rectangles and roll them up like jellyrolls. Form each into a ring. Using scissors, cut through the rings at 1-inch (2.5-cm) intervals, cutting almost to the center. Angle the slices slightly. Place the rings on a buttered pan, cover and let rise in a warm place for about 30 minutes. Bake at 350°F (175°C) for 30 minutes. Cool.

½ cup (120 mL) icing sugar, sifted

2 tsp. (10 mL) light cream

¼ tsp. (1.2 mL) vanilla extract

FOR THE GLAZE: Stir all the ingredients together to make a thick icing. Add more cream if it's too thick. Drizzle over the cooled cake. Store lightly covered at room temperature for up to 2 days.

VARIATION

POPPY SEED COFFEE CAKE: Replace the almond filling with the following:

¾ cup (180 mL) poppy seeds, ground if possible

¾ cup (180 mL) granulated sugar

⅓ cup (80 mL) milk

1 egg, lightly beaten

⅓ cup (80 mL) walnuts, chopped

⅓ cup (80 mL) raisins

2 Tbsp. (30 mL) butter, melted

2 tsp. (10 mL) lemon zest

1 tsp. (5 mL) vanilla extract

½ tsp. (2.5 mL) almond extract

Finely grind the poppy seeds with ¼ cup (60 mL) of the sugar in a blender in 3 batches. (Omit this step if using ground poppy seeds.) Transfer to a medium saucepan and add the remaining ½ cup (120 mL) sugar and milk. Cook over medium heat, stirring constantly, until the sugar dissolves. Remove from the heat and stir in the remaining ingredients. Cool before using. Assemble and bake as with almond filling.

Pumpkin Pecan Coffee Cake

Makes one 10-inch (25-cm) cake (serves 10 to 12)

FOR THE CAKE:

⅔ cup (160 mL) butter, softened

½ cup (120 mL) granulated sugar

⅔ cup (160 mL) brown sugar

3 eggs

1¼ cups (300 mL) pumpkin purée (canned or fresh)

½ cup (120 mL) sour cream

2½ cups (600 mL) all-purpose flour

1½ tsp. (7.5 mL) baking soda

1 tsp. (5 mL) baking powder

½ tsp. (2.5 mL) salt

1½ tsp. (7.5 mL) ground cinnamon

½ tsp. (2.5 mL) ground ginger

1 tsp. (5 mL) ground cloves

½ tsp. (2.5 mL) ground nutmeg

1 cup (240 mL) toasted pecans, coarsely chopped

FOR THE TOPPING:

¾ cup (180 mL) granulated sugar

¼ cup (60 mL) water

¼ cup (60 mL) whipping cream

2 Tbsp. (30 mL) butter

½ tsp. (2.5 mL) vanilla extract

½ cup (120 mL) toasted pecans, coarsely chopped

For all of you who love pumpkin pie and never get enough of your favorite dessert, I came up with a coffee cake that captures the robust flavors and tender texture of fall's most requested pie.

FOR THE CAKE: Preheat the oven to 350°F (175°C). Butter and flour a 10-inch (25-cm) bundt pan.

Using an electric mixer, cream the butter and sugars until light and fluffy. Add the eggs one at a time, beating well after each addition. Combine the pumpkin and sour cream in a separate bowl. Sift the flour, baking soda, baking powder, salt, cinnamon, ginger, cloves and nutmeg together. Add to the egg mixture in 3 parts, alternating with the pumpkin mixture. Stir until just combined. Stir in the pecans. Pour into the prepared pan. Bake for 50 minutes or until a cake tester inserted in the center of the cake comes out clean. Cool for 15 minutes, then remove from the pan.

FOR THE TOPPING: Bring the sugar and water to a boil in a small, heavy saucepan. Swirl the pan to ensure even caramelization. Cook to a medium golden color, without stirring, over medium heat. Remove from the heat. Stirring carefully, add the cream slowly; the mixture will foam. Add the butter and vanilla. Cool until the mixture thickens but can still be poured. Drizzle over the cooled cake and sprinkle with toasted pecans. Store in a tightly closed container at room temperature for up to 3 days.

Pineapple Upside-Down Cake

Make one 10-inch (25-cm) cake (serves 8)

FOR THE TOPPING:

¼ cup (60 mL) butter, melted

½ cup (120 mL) brown sugar

1½ tsp. (7.5 mL) ground cinnamon

6 to 8 pineapple slices

⅓ cup (80 mL) pecans

FOR THE CAKE:

¾ cup (180 mL) butter, softened

1½ cups (360 mL) granulated sugar

3 eggs

1 tsp. (5 mL) vanilla extract

1½ cups (360 mL) all-purpose flour

¾ cup (180 mL) pastry flour

1 Tbsp. (15 mL) baking powder

1¼ tsp. (6.2 mL) baking soda

½ tsp. (2.5 mL) salt

1 cup (240 mL) sour cream

This cake is a sentimental favorite for so many of us, and deservedly so; when made right it is a scrumptious, even elegant, dessert. Traditionally made with pineapple, it is equally delicious made with apricots, plums or any colorful fruit—just substitute 1½ cups (360 mL) of fruit for the pineapple. It is best served slightly warm.

FOR THE TOPPING: Combine the butter, brown sugar and cinnamon. Spread in the bottom of a 10-inch (25-cm) cake pan. Place the pineapple and pecans in a decorative pattern over the brown sugar.

Preheat the oven to 350°F (175°C).

FOR THE CAKE: Using an electric mixer, beat the butter and sugar until light. Add the eggs one at a time, beating well after each addition. Beat in the vanilla. Sift both the flours, baking powder, baking soda and salt together. Add the dry ingredients to the egg mixture in 3 parts, alternating with the sour cream. Spread the batter over the pineapple. Bake for 35 to 40 minutes, or until the cake springs back when lightly pressed in the center. Cool for 10 minutes and then invert onto a serving plate. Serve warm. Store refrigerated in a closed container for up to 2 days.

Orange Bundt Cake

Makes one 10-inch (25-cm) cake (serves 10 to12)

FOR THE CAKE:

1 cup (240 mL) butter, softened

1¼ cups (300 mL) granulated sugar

3 eggs, separated

1 tsp. (5 mL) vanilla extract

1 cup (240 mL) sour cream

4 tsp. (20 mL) orange zest

2 cups (475 mL) all-purpose flour

1 tsp. (5 mL) baking powder

1 tsp. (5 mL) baking soda

½ tsp. (2.5 mL) salt

FOR THE GLAZE:

½ cup (120 mL) orange juice

¼ cup (60 mL) lemon juice

1 cup (240 mL) granulated sugar

2 Tbsp. (30 mL) Grand Marnier (optional)

This is one of those delicate, ladylike cakes that is often served at luncheons, teas and showers. Far too prissy for the guys' Sunday afternoon football spread (give them rocky road brownies—that'll keep them quiet), but perfect with crustless cucumber sandwiches and your best china teacups.

FOR THE CAKE: Preheat the oven to 350°F (175°C). Butter and flour a 10-inch (25-cm) bundt pan.

Using an electric mixer, cream the butter and sugar, beating until light, about 2 minutes. Add the egg yolks and beat until fluffy, about 2 minutes. Add the vanilla, sour cream and orange zest and mix well. Sift the flour, baking powder, baking soda and salt in a separate bowl and add to the mixture. Using an electric mixer, beat the egg whites in another bowl until stiff but not dry. Fold into the batter; do not overbeat. Pour into the prepared pan. Bake about 1 hour, or until a cake tester inserted in the center comes out clean. Leave the cake in the pan on a rack.

FOR THE GLAZE: Combine the orange juice, lemon juice and sugar in a small saucepan over medium heat. Cook until the sugar is dissolved. Stir in the Grand Marnier, if using. Pour half the mixture over the hot cake in the baking pan. Allow it to soak for 15 minutes and then turn the cake out onto a serving plate. Prick with a fork and brush the remaining glaze over the cake. Cool before serving. Store in a tightly closed container at room temperature for up to 4 days.

Lemon Pudding Cake

Makes one 9-inch (23-cm) square cake or 6 individual portions

½ cup (120 mL) pastry flour

½ cup (120 mL) granulated sugar

½ tsp. (2.5 mL) salt

3 eggs at room temperature, separated

1 cup (240 mL) fresh lemon juice

1 Tbsp. (15 mL) lemon zest

1 tsp. (5 mL) vanilla extract

¼ cup (60 mL) butter, melted

1¼ cups (300 mL) milk or half-and-half

¼ cup (60 mL) granulated sugar

I made this dessert for the first time in home economics class in grade 7; it made such an impression on me that even at that tender age I vowed to include it if I ever wrote a cookbook. Since I didn't have my original recipe, I searched high and low through many old cookbooks. The recipes I discovered were all basically the same, with some slight variation in the proportions of ingredients. What I love about this dessert is that, as if by magic, it separates into a tender cake layer on top and a luscious pudding on the bottom. It bakes up wonderfully in a single pan or in individual portions for a more elegant presentation. Decrease the amount of lemon juice if you want a sweeter pudding. Use milk instead of cream for a less rich version. Serve it warm with lightly sweetened whipped cream

Preheat the oven to 350°F (175°C). Butter a 9-inch (23-cm) square cake pan or six 3-inch (7.5-cm) ovenproof cups or ramekins.

Combine the flour, ½ cup (120 mL) sugar and salt. In another bowl, beat the egg yolks until smooth. Stir in the lemon juice and zest, vanilla, butter and milk or half-and-half. Beat the egg whites to form soft peaks. Gradually beat in the ¼ cup (60 mL) sugar and continue beating until stiff, moist peaks form. Fold the egg whites into the lemon mixture.

Pour into the prepared pan or cups. Set the pan or cups into a large pan filled with 1 inch (2.5 cm) of hot water. Bake for 40 to 50 minutes for the pan, 15 to 20 minutes for the cups. Serve warm or at room temperature.

Hot Fudge Pudding Cake

Makes one 9-inch (23-cm) square cake or 8 individual servings

1 cup (240 mL) all-purpose
   flour
¾ cup (180 mL) granulated
   sugar
½ cup (120 mL) cocoa
   (preferably Dutch-process)
2 tsp. (10 mL) baking powder
¼ tsp. (1.2 mL) salt
½ cup (120 mL) milk
¼ cup (60 mL) butter, melted
1 tsp. (5 mL) vanilla extract
¾ cup (180 mL) brown sugar
½ cup (120 mL) walnuts,
   chopped
1 ½ cups (360 mL) hot water

If you are not familiar with this version of the magic pudding cake, you are in for a surprise. Imagine plopping a simple cake batter into a pan, pouring hot water over it, and then, like magic, a luscious squishy pudding appears, topped with moist chocolate cake. Served with whipped cream or vanilla ice cream, it's comfort food at its best—or, with another wave of your magic wand, an elegant dessert served in individual ramekins, with crème anglaise or fresh raspberries.

Preheat the oven to 350°F (175°C). Butter a 9-inch (23-cm) cake pan or eight 3-inch (7.5-cm) ovenproof cups or ramekins.

Combine the flour, sugar, ¼ cup (60 mL) of the cocoa, baking powder and salt in a medium bowl. Mix thoroughly with a wooden spoon. Add the milk, melted butter and vanilla and stir well. Pour the batter into the prepared pan or cups.

Mix together the brown sugar, walnuts and remaining ¼ cup (60 mL) cocoa. Sprinkle over the batter. Carefully pour hot water over top. Do not stir. Bake for 30 to 45 minutes for a 9-inch (23-cm) pan, 15 to 20 minutes for cups. Serve warm.

Lemon Bread

Makes one 9-inch (23-cm) loaf (serves 8)

FOR THE BREAD:

½ cup (120 mL) butter, softened

1 cup (240 mL) granulated sugar

1 tsp. (5 mL) vanilla extract

2 eggs

1 ¾ cups (420 mL) all-purpose flour

1 ½ tsp. (7.5 mL) baking powder

½ tsp. (2.5 mL) baking soda

½ tsp. (2.5 mL) salt

⅔ cup (160 mL) milk

⅓ cup (80 mL) lemon juice

1 Tbsp. (15 mL) lemon zest

FOR THE GLAZE:

⅓ cup (80 mL) granulated sugar

¼ cup (60 mL) lemon juice

Simple and homey, with a delightfully moist and tender texture, this tangy glazed bread is a perfect tea-time treat.

FOR THE BREAD: Preheat the oven to 325°F (165°C). Butter and flour a 9 x 5 x 3-inch (23 x 12.5 x 7.5-cm) loaf pan.

Using an electric mixer, cream the butter and sugar until light. Add the vanilla and eggs and beat until fluffy. Stir together the flour, baking powder, baking soda and salt. Add the dry ingredients to the butter mixture in 3 parts, alternating with the milk and lemon juice. Mix until smooth. Stir in the lemon zest. Spread in the prepared pan. Bake for 50 to 60 minutes, or until a cake tester inserted in the center comes out clean.

FOR THE GLAZE: In a small saucepan over medium heat, combine the sugar and lemon juice. Heat until the mixture bubbles and the sugar dissolves, stirring occasionally. Pour over the warm loaf in the pan. Allow to cool for 15 minutes. Turn the loaf out and cool on a rack. Wrap with plastic and store at room temperature for up to 5 days.

VARIATION

BERRY LEMON LOAF: Fold 1 cup (240 mL) wild blueberries or raspberries into the batter just before turning it into the pan, or replace the lemon zest with orange zest and fold in 1 cup (240 mL) cranberries just before turning the batter into the pan.

Date Pecan Scones

Makes 12 to 18 scones

1 cup (240 mL) cold butter,
  cut into ½-inch (1.2-cm)
  pieces

1⅔ cups (400 mL) pastry
  flour

3 cups (720 mL) all-purpose
  flour

¾ cup (180 mL) golden
  brown sugar

½ tsp. (2.5 mL) salt

2 tsp. (10 mL) baking powder

¾ tsp. (3.6 mL) baking soda

1 cup (240 mL) chopped
  pecans

1 cup (240 mL) chopped dates

1¼ cups (300 mL) half-and-
  half

1 tsp. (5 mL) vanilla extract

cream and sugar, for brushing

"Scones? I've eaten scones and I don't particularly like them; they're kind of boring." You will eat those words immediately after you've tasted these babies—just ask the loyal fans at our café. For me, a perfect scone is crispy, almost brittle on the outside, and soft and tender on the inside, with just enough sweetness to stand on its own (although even the perfect scone is even more so served warm with preserves—apricot or raspberry being my preferred choices). The food processor was invented for this recipe. You'll have scones in the oven in 15 minutes and on the table in another 20.

Preheat the oven to 350°F (175°C). Line a 12 x 18-inch (30 x 45-cm) baking sheet with parchment paper.

Place the butter, both flours, sugar, salt, baking powder and baking soda into the bowl of a food processor (or use a pastry blender). Process until the mixture is very fine. Transfer to a large bowl and add the pecans and dates. Pour the cream and vanilla over top. Mix with a fork until a crumbly dough forms.

Turn onto a work surface. Press the mixture together very lightly—it should be fairly dry. Cut into twelve 2½-inch (6.2-cm) rounds or eighteen 1½-inch (3.8-cm) rounds. Place on the prepared pan. Brush with cream and sprinkle with sugar. Bake for 20 to 25 minutes until golden. Serve warm. Scones are best served the day they are made, but they can be stored lightly covered at room temperature for up to 2 days. Reheat before serving.

VARIATIONS

APRICOT ALMOND SCONES: Substitute apricots for the dates, almonds for the pecans and ½ tsp. (2.5 mL) almond extract for the vanilla.

PEAR GINGER SCONES: Substitute 1½ cups (360 mL) chopped pears for the dates, omit the nuts and add 2 Tbsp. (30 mL) finely chopped candied ginger.

Butter Tarts

FOR THE CRUST:

1 cup (240 mL) cold butter, cut into ½-inch (1.2-cm) pieces

2½ cups (600 mL) all-purpose flour

¼ cup (60 mL) granulated sugar

¼ tsp. (1.2 mL) salt

⅓ cup (80 mL) water

FOR THE FILLING:

2 eggs

1 cup (240 mL) brown sugar

¾ cup (180 mL) corn syrup

1 tsp. (5 mL) vinegar

1 tsp. (5 mL) vanilla extract

¼ tsp. (1.2 mL) salt

½ cup (120 mL) melted butter

½ cup (120 mL) raisins, soaked in hot water for 15 minutes and drained

½ cup (120 mL) chopped walnuts

I know they are a Canadian tradition, but really, haven't we seen enough recipes for butter tarts? But when was the last time you had a perfect butter tart—with tender, flaky pastry and an achingly sweet buttery filling that drizzled down your chin? I rest my case. Except for your grandmother's, these are the world's best butter tarts. The operative word here is "butter" and lots of it, in the crust, in the filling and on your hands and chin after you've eaten one—or more likely two—of these little morsels.

FOR THE CRUST: Using a food processor or a pastry cutter and a large bowl, combine the butter, flour, sugar and salt and process or cut in until the mixture beings to clump. Add the water and combine just until the dough holds together. Press the dough to form a disk, wrap in plastic and refrigerate for 20 minutes.

Roll out the pastry and cut 3¾-inch (9-cm) rounds to fit 2½-inch (6.2-cm) tart tins with a slight overhang. Fit the pastry into the tins and refrigerate for 10 to 15 minutes.

FOR THE FILLING: Using an electric mixer or a whisk, combine the eggs, sugar, corn syrup, vinegar, vanilla and salt. Beat until well combined, but not frothy. Stir in the melted butter.

Preheat the oven to 350°F (175°C). Sprinkle the raisins and nuts evenly in the prepared tart shells. Pour the filling into the shells, almost to the top. Bake for 15 to 20 minutes, or until the filling is just set and the crust is golden. Cool before removing from the tins. Store at room temperature for up to 4 days.

VARIATION

PECAN TARTS: Substitute 1 cup (240 mL) whole pecans for the raisins and chopped walnuts.

Chocolate Pecan Tarts

Makes 2 dozen tarts

FOR THE CRUST:

1 cup (240 mL) cold butter, cut into ½-inch (1.2-cm) pieces

2¼ cups (535 mL) all-purpose flour

⅔ cup (160 mL) cocoa

1¼ cups (300 mL) icing sugar

¼ tsp. (1.2 mL) salt

⅓ cup (80 mL) water

FOR THE FILLING:

2 eggs

1 cup (240 mL) brown sugar

¾ cup (180 mL) corn syrup

1 tsp. (5 mL) vinegar

1 tsp. (5 mL) vanilla extract

¼ tsp. (1.2 mL) salt

½ cup (120 mL) melted butter

1 cup (240 mL) whole pecans

FOR THE TOPPING:

½ cup (120 mL) whipping cream

4 oz. (113 g) semisweet chocolate, coarsely chopped

1 Tbsp. (15 mL) corn syrup

Be forewarned, these tarts constitute a serious threat to your self-restraint. Some desserts present natural obstacles to temptation—they require cutting, plating, heating or chilling before they can be devoured. These tarts are dangerous; they just sit there looking gooey, chocolatey and absolutely inviting. They are the perfect size to eat in three bites, but after you've tried one, three bites will not be enough.

FOR THE CRUST: Using a food processor or a pastry cutter and a large bowl, combine the butter, flour, cocoa, icing sugar and salt and process or cut in until the mixture begins to clump. Add the water and combine just until the dough holds together. Press to form a disk, wrap in plastic and refrigerate for 20 minutes.

Roll out the pastry and cut 3¾-inch (9-cm) rounds to fit 2½-inch (6.2-cm) tart tins with a slight overhang. Fit the pastry into the tins and refrigerate for 10 to 15 minutes.

FOR THE FILLING: Using an electric mixer or a whisk, combine the eggs, sugar, corn syrup, vinegar, vanilla and salt. Beat until well combined, but not frothy. Stir in the melted butter.

Preheat the oven to 350°F (175°C). Sprinkle the pecans evenly over the prepared tart shells. Pour the filling into the shells, almost to the top. Bake for 15 to 20 minutes, or until the filling is just set and the crust is crispy. Cool before topping.

FOR THE TOPPING: Heat the cream in a small saucepan over medium heat or in the microwave until bubbly. Remove from heat and stir in the chocolate and corn syrup. Mix until smooth. Allow to cool until slightly thickened. Dot the tops of the cooled tarts with the chocolate and swirl to partially cover the pecans. Allow to set before removing the tarts to a serving dish. Store at room temperature for up to 4 days.

Marzipan Raspberry Tarts

Makes 2 dozen tarts

FOR THE CRUST:

1 cup (240 mL) cold butter, cut into $\frac{1}{2}$-inch (1.2-cm) pieces

2$\frac{1}{2}$ cups (600 mL) all-purpose flour

$\frac{1}{4}$ cup (60 mL) granulated sugar

$\frac{1}{4}$ tsp. (1.2 mL) salt

$\frac{1}{3}$ cup (80 mL) water

FOR THE FILLING:

$\frac{2}{3}$ cup (160 mL) butter, softened

$\frac{3}{4}$ cup (180 mL) granulated sugar

4 egg yolks

1 tsp. (5 mL) almond extract

2 cups (475 mL) ground almonds

1 cup (240 mL) raspberry jam

icing sugar, for dusting

I have a particular weakness for almonds; I love their delicate texture, their slightly perfumed taste, and their surprising ability to complement so many other ingredients—in this case, raspberries. Although they do not contain actual marzipan, these seductive little tarts have the same tender, fragrant softness, with the added surprise of raspberry jam hidden below.

FOR THE CRUST: Using a food processor or a pastry cutter and a large bowl, combine the butter, flour, sugar and salt and process or cut in until the mixture begins to clump. Add the water and combine just until the dough holds together. Press to form a disk, wrap in plastic and refrigerate for 20 minutes. Roll out the pastry and cut 3$\frac{3}{4}$-inch (9-cm) rounds to fit 2$\frac{1}{2}$-inch (6.2-cm) tart tins with a slight overhang. Fit into the tins and refrigerate for 10 to 15 minutes.

FOR THE FILLING: Using an electric mixer or a wooden spoon, cream the butter with the sugar. Add the egg yolks and beat until light and creamy, about 2 to 3 minutes. Add the almond extract and ground almonds. Beat to combine thoroughly.

Preheat the oven to 350°F (175°C). Divide the jam among the tart shells. Spoon the filling into the shells and smooth the tops. Bake for 20 to 25 minutes, or until the filling is set and pale golden. Cool and dust with icing sugar. Store at room temperature in a tightly covered container for up to 5 days.

Luv Muffins

Makes 2 dozen muffins

FOR THE MUFFINS:

½ cup (120 mL) butter

1⅔ cups (400 mL) granulated sugar

3 eggs

1 tsp. (5 mL) vanilla extract

1 cup (240 mL) all-purpose flour

1 cup (240 mL) pastry flour

½ tsp. (2.5 mL) baking powder

1¼ tsp. (6.2 mL) baking soda

¼ tsp. (1.2 mL) salt

2 cups (475 mL) cocoa

1⅓ cups (320 mL) cold water

1½ cups (360 mL) cream cheese, softened

1¼ cups (300 mL) icing sugar

½ tsp. (2.5 mL) vanilla extract

¼ tsp. (1.2 mL) almond extract

This recipe was inspired by my dear friend and first employee Basia Krzyzanowski. Way back in the early years of my business our repertoire of desserts consisted solely of pies, but on occasional mornings Basia would whip up muffins for our coffee break. She is a naturally gifted baker and cook and anything she makes is always delicious, but somehow these muffins were supernaturally good, as if enchanted. Every day Basia would delight us with her ambrosial treats, and then, just as suddenly as it began, the magic ended; one day the enchanted muffins were, sadly, just muffins. As it turns out, the magic of these muffins depended entirely on Basia being in love, and when the bloom was off the rose, alas, cupid's love muffins became mere mortal fare. Fortunately for us, Basia fell in love often. We first offered these chocolate cupcakes on Valentine's Day, appropriately enough, and decorated them with a white chocolate squiggle in the shape of a heart.

FOR THE MUFFINS: Preheat the oven to 350°F (175°C). Butter and line 12 muffin cups with paper liners.

Using an electric mixer, cream the butter and sugar until fluffy, about 2 minutes. Add the eggs and vanilla and beat until light. Sift both the flours, baking powder, baking soda and salt in a separate bowl. Combine the cocoa with the water and whisk until smooth. Add the flour mixture to the butter mixture alternately with the cocoa. Beat until smooth. Fill the muffin cups half full with the batter.

Using an electric mixer or a wooden spoon, beat the cream cheese, icing sugar, vanilla and almond extract until light and smooth. Drop by tablespoons into the half-filled muffin tins. Top with the remaining batter, filling the cups almost to the top. Bake for 15 to 20 minutes, until the tops spring back when pressed. Do not use a cake tester. Cool in the pans for 20 minutes before removing to a rack and cooling completely.

FOR THE GLAZE:

¾ cup (180 mL) butter

8 oz. (225 g) semisweet
chocolate, coarsely chopped

½ cup (120 mL) whipping
cream

2 Tbsp. (30 mL) corn syrup

2 oz. (57 g) white chocolate,
coarsely chopped

FOR THE GLAZE: Melt the butter and chocolate in a medium saucepan over low heat or in the microwave, stirring occasionally. Stir in the cream and syrup. Cool until slightly thickened. Dip the tops of the muffins in the glaze and chill until set. Melt the white chocolate in a double boiler over hot water or in the microwave. Place the chocolate in a pastry bag or paper cone. Pipe a squiggle of your choice on the top of each muffin. Store in a closed container at room temperature for up to 3 days.

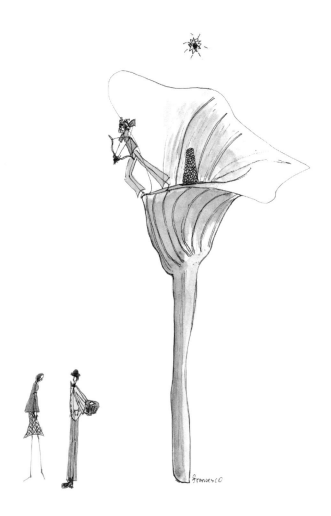

Maple Pecan Sticky Buns

Makes 16 to 20 buns

FOR THE DOUGH:

¼ cup (60 mL) warm water (105° to 115°F/40° to 45°C)

2 packages active dry yeast (4½ tsp./22 mL)

⅓ cup (80 mL) granulated sugar

1 cup (240 mL) sour cream

2 eggs, beaten

1 tsp. (5 mL) vanilla extract

4 cups (950 mL) all-purpose flour

½ tsp. (2.5 mL) salt

½ cup (120 mL) butter, softened

FOR THE FILLING:

½ cup (120 mL) butter, softened

½ cup (120 mL) brown sugar

1 Tbsp. (15 mL) ground cinnamon

1 cup (240 mL) raisins (optional)

FOR THE MAPLE PECAN LAYER:

½ cup (120 mL) butter

1 cup (240 mL) brown sugar

1 cup (240 mL) maple syrup

1 tsp. (5 mL) vanilla extract

1½ cups (360 mL) pecans

The operative word here is "sticky," and I say, the stickier the better. I urge you not to dwell on the amount of butter, sour cream, sticky syrup and brown sugar that goes into these gooey buns. Push on, get them in the oven and into your mouth, and then you won't care. If you want to exercise some restraint (or, more likely, if you can't wait to eat them) skip the cream cheese drizzle—they really don't need it.

FOR THE DOUGH: Place the water in a large bowl; add the yeast and 1 Tbsp. (15 mL) of the sugar. Stir and allow to sit for 5 minutes, until bubbly, then stir in the rest of the sugar. Combine the sour cream, eggs and vanilla. Stir into the yeast mixture. Beat in the flour and salt until well combined. Add the butter and beat until the dough is smooth, about 3 to 4 minutes. Place the dough in a well-buttered bowl. Cover and allow to rest at least 2 hours at room temperature, or up to 2 days refrigerated.

Divide the dough in half. Roll each piece on a floured board to approximately ½-inch (1.2-cm) thickness, forming a rectangle about 9 x 12 inches (23 x 30 cm).

FOR THE FILLING: Combine the butter, brown sugar and cinnamon; add the raisins. Spread the filling equally over each rectangle and roll it up lengthwise. Cut each roll into 8 equal sections.

FOR THE MAPLE PECAN LAYER: Melt the butter in a small saucepan over medium-low heat. Stir in the sugar until it has dissolved. Add the maple syrup and simmer for 5 minutes. Generously butter two 10-inch (25-cm) cake pans. Stir the vanilla into the syrup mixture. Pour into the prepared pans and sprinkle with the pecans.

FOR THE GLAZE:

½ cup (120 mL) cream cheese

1 cup (240 mL) icing sugar

½ tsp. (2.5 mL) vanilla
  extract

milk

Arrange the sticky bun sections evenly in the prepared pans. Cover lightly and let rise for ½ to 1 hour, depending on the warmth of the room.

Preheat the oven to 350°F (175°C). Bake for 25 to 30 minutes. Allow to cool for 5 minutes and then invert onto a serving plate. Cool for 15 minutes.

FOR THE GLAZE: Combine the cream cheese, icing sugar and vanilla. Add enough milk to make a pourable icing. Drizzle the glaze over the warm buns. Serve warm or at room temperature. Store lightly covered at room temperature for up to 1 day.

Chocolate Hazelnut Biscotti

Makes 3 dozen biscotti

4 eggs

¼ cup (60 mL) vegetable oil

2 tsp. (10 mL) vanilla extract

1¼ cups (300 mL) granulated sugar

1½ cups (360 mL) all-purpose flour

¾ cup (180 mL) cocoa

2 tsp. (10 mL) baking powder

½ tsp. (2.5 mL) baking soda

½ tsp. (2.5 mL) salt

¾ cup (180 mL) finely ground toasted hazelnuts

¾ cup (180 mL) whole toasted hazelnuts

1 cup (240 mL) coarsely chopped semisweet chocolate

1 egg, beaten

¼ cup (60 mL) sugar

Wait, don't turn the page, this is not a recipe for those jaw-breaking projectiles made of compressed sawdust that you dunk in your coffee and then pretend to eat. Quite the contrary. For those of you who have always thought of eating biscotti as a chore, somewhat more enjoyable than, say, doing laundry, but still basically a waste of time, I have biscotti that you will actually neglect to dunk and eat straight, no chaser. Intensely chocolate, with crunchy flavorful hazelnuts for visual and textural contrast, these biscotti will make converts of us all.

Preheat the oven to 325°F (165oC). Line a 12 x 18-inch (30 x 45-cm) baking sheet with parchment paper.

Whisk the 4 eggs, oil and vanilla lightly, about 60 seconds. Combine the 1¼ cups (300 mL) sugar, flour, cocoa, baking powder, baking soda, salt, ground nuts, whole nuts, and chocolate in a large bowl. Add the beaten eggs in 2 batches, combining thoroughly with a wooden spoon.

Turn out onto a lightly floured surface. Divide in half and form two 12 x 2-inch (30 x 5-cm) logs. Place the logs on the baking sheet. Brush with the beaten egg and sprinkle with the ¼ cup (60 mL) sugar. Bake for 30 to 35 minutes. Remove from the oven and let rest for 30 minutes.

Reduce the temperature to 300°F (150°C). Cut the logs into ½-inch (1.2-cm) slices. Place the slices on the baking sheet and bake for 25 to 30 minutes. Cool to room temperature. Store in a tightly closed container for up to 3 weeks.

Cinnamon Pecan Rugelach,
page 104

Clockwise from top: Butterscotch Brownies, page 108; Skor Brownies, page 110; White Chocolate Brownies, page 112

Luv Muffins,
page 140

Rustic Pear Tarts,
page 145

Rustic Pear Tarts

Makes 1½ dozen tarts

FOR THE PASTRY:

1 cup (240 mL) cold butter, cut into ½-inch (1.2-cm) pieces

2⅓ cups (560 mL) all-purpose flour

¼ tsp. (1.2 mL) salt

⅓ cup (80 mL) granulated sugar

1½ cups (360 mL) pecans, very finely chopped

1 tsp. (5 mL) vanilla extract

2 egg yolks

3 Tbsp. (45 mL) cold water

FOR THE FILLING:

¾ cup (180 mL) brown sugar

2 Tbsp. (30 mL) all-purpose flour

1 tsp. (5 mL) ground cinnamon

3 Tbsp. (45 mL) butter, melted

12 ripe medium pears, with stems

1 cup (240 mL) pecans, slightly broken up

½ cup (120 mL) apricot jam or apple jelly

These darling little miniature pear tarts were inspired by our large Rustic Pear Pie (page 50), which was in turn inspired by our pear dumplings. I cannot get enough of pears and when asked to make dessert for 800 guests at an organic farmers' fundraiser, I wanted to prepare a dessert that was eye-catching, easy to serve and celebrated the bounty of Ontario's autumn harvest.

FOR THE PASTRY: Using a food processor or pastry blender, process or cut the butter into the flour, salt and sugar until the mixture resembles fine meal. Add the pecans, vanilla, egg yolks and water. Gently mix until just combined. Form into two disks, cover in plastic wrap and chill for 20 to 30 minutes. Roll out the pastry and cut 4¼-inch (10.5 cm) rounds to fit 3-inch (7.5-cm) tart tins with a slight overhang.

Preheat the oven to 325°F (165°C).

FOR THE FILLING: Combine the sugar, flour, cinnamon and melted butter until crumbly. Sprinkle about ¼ of the mixture on the bottom of the prepared tart shells.

Peel the pears, leaving the stems attached. Slice off the bottom ⅓ of each pear and reserve. Remove any seeds from the top section and trim the bottom to resemble a pear shape. Reserve ¼ cup (60 mL) of the crumble mixture for the last 6 tarts. Roll the pears in the remaining crumb mixture and stand them up in 12 of the prepared shells. Distribute ⅔ of the pecans around the pears and sprinkle with more of the crumb mixture.

Cut up the reserved pear pieces and fill the remaining 6 tart shells. Place the remaining pecans over the pear pieces and sprinkle with the last of the crumble.

Bake for 20 to 25 minutes, or until the crumble is golden brown. Cool slightly. Warm the jam or jelly and brush it over the tarts. Serve warm or at room temperature. Store lightly covered at room temperature for up to 2 days.

Caramelized Banana Bread Pudding

Makes one 9 x 13-inch (23 x 33-cm) pan (serves 10 to 12)

FOR THE CARAMELIZED BANANAS:

3 Tbsp. (45 mL) butter

⅓ cup (80 mL) brown sugar

4 bananas

1 Tbsp. (15 mL) rum

FOR THE BREAD MIXTURE:

8 cups (2 L) stale French bread cut into 1-inch (2.5-cm) cubes

1 cup (240 mL) pecans

1 cup (240 mL) raisins

1 cup (240 mL) sweetened shredded coconut

3 eggs

1 cup (240 mL) granulated sugar

½ cup (120 mL) brown sugar

2 tsp. (10 mL) vanilla extract

¼ cup (60 mL) rum

1 tsp. (5 mL) ground cinnamon

1 tsp. (5 mL) ground nutmeg

½ tsp. (2.5 mL) salt

3 cups (720 mL) milk

1 cup (240 mL) whipping cream

½ cup (120 mL) butter, melted

FOR THE RUM SAUCE:

½ cup (120 mL) butter

2 egg yolks

1½ cups (360 mL) icing sugar

½ cup (120 mL) rum

I love all bread puddings, but I do have a particular fondness for the more southern, Louisiana-style puddings, chock-full of pecans, raisins and cinnamon and, of course, served with the requisite bourbon sauce. Here, the traditional southern ingredients are in great company with coconut, rum and caramelized bananas, creating a comfy dessert with a decisively tropical twist.

Butter a 9 x 13-inch (23 x 33-cm) deep baking dish. Melt the butter with ⅓ cup (80 mL) brown sugar in a heavy skillet. Cook over medium heat, stirring occasionally, until the sugar begins to caramelize, about 3 minutes. Slice the bananas and add to the pan. Stir gently for about 3 to 4 minutes. Remove from the heat and drizzle with the rum. Cool slightly and then spread in the prepared pan.

Preheat the oven to 350°F (175°C). In a large bowl combine the bread, pecans, raisins and coconut. Spread the bread mixture over the bananas. Whisk the eggs and sugars together in a medium bowl until smooth and frothy. Stir in the vanilla, rum, cinnamon, nutmeg, salt, milk, cream and melted butter. Pour the egg mixture over the bread layer and press slightly to flatten. Bake for approximately 1 hour or until set in the center and the top is starting to brown.

FOR THE RUM SAUCE: Melt the butter in a heavy saucepan over low heat. Whisk the egg yolks and icing sugar together. Stir into the melted butter. Cook over medium heat, stirring constantly, until slightly thickened, about 3 minutes. Remove from the heat. Cool slightly, then stir in the rum.

Scoop the warm pudding into serving bowls and serve with the sauce. Store in the refrigerator covered for up to 2 days. Reheat before serving.

Cheesecakes

Do a quick survey among your friends and co-workers and you'll find that the world is divided into "pie" lovers and "cheesecake" lovers. Some may sit on the fence, but when pressed will give you an answer in a split second. Although my loyalties lie unabashedly in the pie camp, I must confess I am always searching for the perfect cheesecake. Being a devotee of pies, in all their delicate, juicy glory, I am often dismayed by the denseness and stodginess of some cheesecakes. A cheesecake should be delicate, silky and not overly sugary. The tenderly crisp crust should balance the creamy firmness of the filling, and the topping—whether fruit, mousse or chocolate—should add another dimension to the whole scrumptious experience.

Cappuccino Cheesecake

Makes one 10-inch (25-cm) cake (serves 12 to 14)

FOR THE CRUST:

1 ¾ cups (420 mL) chocolate
  wafer crumbs

⅓ cup (80 mL) butter, melted
  and hot

1 Tbsp. (15 mL) granulated
  sugar

FOR THE FILLING:

1 ½ lb. (680 g) cream cheese,
  softened

1 ¼ cups (300 mL) granulated
  sugar

5 eggs, room temperature

2 Tbsp. (30 mL) instant coffee
  granules

2 Tbsp. (30 mL) hot water

2 Tbsp. (30 mL) vanilla
  extract

3 Tbsp. (45 mL) all-purpose
  flour

¾ cup (180 mL) whipping
  cream

6 oz. (170 g) semisweet
  chocolate, coarsely chopped

¼ cup (60 mL) whipping
  cream

This is a serious piece of work—dark, dense, and slightly bitter. If you have a love affair with coffee and dark chocolate like I do, these words will not scare you off. On the contrary, you will agree that the velvety smoothness of the cream cheese, the intense bitterness of the coffee and chocolate, and the sweet crunchiness of the crust are the perfect combination, creating an extraordinarily satisfying cheesecake.

FOR THE CRUST: Preheat the oven to 350°F (175°C). Combine the crust ingredients in a small bowl, mixing well. Press into the bottom and up the sides of a 10-inch (25-cm) springform pan. Bake for 8 minutes.

FOR THE FILLING: Using an electric mixer, beat the cream cheese and sugar until smooth and light, about 5 minutes. Beat in the eggs, one at a time. Dissolve the coffee in the hot water and add to the cheese mixture. Stir in the vanilla, flour and ¾ cup (180 mL) cream, mixing until blended. Pour half the mixture in the prepared crust.

Melt the chocolate with the ¼ cup (60 mL) cream in a small saucepan over low heat or in the microwave. Stir until smooth. Spoon half the mixture over the batter in the pan. Pour in the rest of the batter. Spoon the remaining chocolate mixture over the batter and swirl with a knife. Bake for 15 minutes. Reduce the heat to 225°F (105°C) and bake for 1 hour, until the cake is set in the center but still soft. Cool completely before topping.

3 Tbsp. (45 mL) granulated
sugar

¾ cup (180 mL) sour cream

1 Tbsp. (15 mL) instant coffee
granules

1 tsp. (5 mL) vanilla extract

½ cup (120 mL) whipping
cream

8 oz. (225 g) semisweet
chocolate, coarsely chopped

1 Tbsp. (15 mL) corn syrup

FOR THE TOPPING: Remove the cheesecake from the pan and place on a serving plate. In a small bowl, combine the sugar, sour cream, coffee and vanilla. Stir until the sugar and coffee are completely dissolved.

Heat the cream in a small saucepan over medium heat until just boiling. Stir in the chocolate, remove from the heat and let sit for 5 minutes. Stir until melted and smooth. Stir in the corn syrup. Cool to lukewarm. Remove ½ cup (120 mL) and chill for 10 to 15 minutes. Add the remainder to the sour cream mixture, stirring until well blended. Spoon most of the chilled chocolate mixture (it should be starting to thicken but still be glossy) into a piping bag with a medium star tip. Pipe a decorative border around the edge of the cheesecake. Spoon the sour cream mixture inside the border. Heat any remaining chocolate mixture and drizzle over the top of the cake. Store refrigerated in a closed container for up to 4 days.

Mango Chiffon Cheesecake

Makes one 10-inch (25-cm) cake (serves 12 to 14)

FOR THE CRUST:

1¼ cups (300 mL) graham cracker crumbs

¾ cup (180 mL) coconut

⅓ cup (80 mL) butter, melted and hot

1 Tbsp. (15 mL) granulated sugar

½ tsp. (2.5 mL) vanilla extract

FOR THE FILLING:

1½ lb. (680 mL) cream cheese, softened

1¼ cups (300 mL) granulated sugar

5 eggs

2 tsp. (10 mL) vanilla extract

2 Tbsp. (30 mL) all-purpose flour

2 tsp. (10 mL) lemon zest

¾ cup (180 mL) whipping cream

½ cup (120 mL) strained mango purée

As reluctant as I am to pick favorites, when it come to cheesecake, this one edges out the competition by a nose. What could be more divine than tart mango purée swirled into a velvety smooth cream cheese filling, topped with tangy mousse and a luminescent mango glaze?

FOR THE CRUST: Preheat the oven to 350°F (175°C).

Combine the crust ingredients in a small bowl, mixing well. Press into the bottom and sides of a 10-inch (25-cm) springform pan. Bake for 8 minutes. Reduce the heat to 225°F (105°C).

FOR THE FILLING: Using an electric mixer, beat the cream cheese and sugar until smooth and light, about 5 minutes. Beat in the eggs, one at a time. Add the remaining ingredients, mixing until just blended. Pour the mixture into the prepared crust. Bake for 60 minutes, or until the cake is set but still soft in the center. Cool.

Secrets of the Perfect Cheesecake

To guarantee a creamy, evenly textured cake, make sure all your ingredients are at room temperature. Overbeating and overbaking can create cracks in your finished cheesecake. After adding the eggs, beat on low, and for a short time only. Make sure your baking instructions call for a low baking temperature and remove the cake from the oven when the cake is firm and no longer shiny. Cheesecakes are best baked at least one day in advance to allow the flavors to mellow.

FOR THE MOUSSE:

1 ¼ cups (300 mL) strained
mango purée

1 package gelatin (2 ¼ tsp./
11 mL)

2 cups (475 mL) whipping
cream

1 tsp. (5 mL) vanilla extract

¼ to ½ cup (60 to 120 mL)
granulated sugar (depend-
ing on sweetness of mangos)

FOR THE GLAZE:

¾ cup (180 mL) strained
mango purée

1 tsp. (5 mL) cornstarch

3 Tbsp. (45 mL) granulated
sugar

FOR THE MOUSSE: Place ¼ cup (60 mL) of the mango purée in a small saucepan. Sprinkle the gelatin over top, let it sit for 5 minutes and then heat gently over low heat until the gelatin is dissolved. Remove from the heat and stir the mixture grad-ually into the remaining 1 cup (240 mL) purée. Chill until it is starting to thicken, stirring occasionally.

Using an electric mixer and a chilled bowl, beat the cream, vanilla and sugar until stiff peaks form. Fold in the cooled mango purée, mixing until smooth.

FOR THE GLAZE: Combine the mango purée, cornstarch and sugar and in a small saucepan. Cook over medium heat until the mixture comes to a boil. Boil for ½ minute. Cool to lukewarm.

TO ASSEMBLE: Remove the cheesecake from the pan and place on a serving plate. Spread ¾ of the mango mousse evenly over the cake, all the way to the edges. Spoon the remainder of the mousse into a pastry bag with a large tip and pipe a decorative border around the outside edge of the cake. Spoon the glaze over the top of the mousse. Tilt the cake to spread the glaze evenly. Chill until set. Store refrigerated in a closed container for up to 4 days.

VARIATION

STRAWBERRY CHIFFON CHEESECAKE: Substitute half strained puréed strawberries and half strawberry jam for the mango purée. Reduce the sugar according to the sweetness of the berries.

Lemon Chiffon Cheesecake

Makes one 10-inch (25-cm) cake (serves 12 to 14)

FOR THE CRUST:

1¼ cups (300 mL) graham cracker crumbs

¾ cup (180 mL) finely chopped almonds

⅓ cup (80 mL) butter, melted and hot

2 Tbsp. (30 mL) granulated sugar

¼ tsp. (1.2 mL) almond extract

FOR THE FILLING:

1½ lb. (680 g) cream cheese, softened

1¼ cups (300 mL) granulated sugar

5 eggs

2 Tbsp. (30 mL) vanilla extract

3 Tbsp. (45 mL) all-purpose flour

⅓ cup (80 mL) lemon juice

1 Tbsp. (15 mL) lemon zest

1 cup (240 mL) sour cream

Although not a chiffon in the true sense, since it does not contain beaten egg whites, the billowy mousse topping captures the airy essence of chiffon. Lemons add a freshness to this cheesecake, which, although velvety rich and creamy, sits lightly even after an extravagant meal.

FOR THE CRUST: Preheat the oven to 350°F (175°C).

Combine the crust ingredients in a small bowl, mixing well. Press into the bottom and up the sides of a 10-inch (25-cm) springform pan. Bake for 8 minutes. Remove and reduce the oven temperature to 225°F (105°C).

FOR THE FILLING: Using an electric mixer, beat the cream cheese and sugar until smooth and light, about 5 minutes. Beat in the eggs one at a time. Add the vanilla, flour, lemon juice, lemon zest and sour cream, mixing until just blended. Pour into the prepared crust and bake for 60 minutes, or until the cake is just set in the center, but still soft. Cool.

FOR THE TOPPING:

1 package (2¼ tsp./11 mL)
  gelatin

1 Tbsp. (15 mL) water

2 cups (475 mL) whipping
  cream

½ tsp. (2.5 mL) vanilla extract

1 cup (240 mL) Lemon Curd
  (see page 216)

2 Tbsp. (30 mL) lemon juice

FOR THE TOPPING: Combine the gelatin and water in a small saucepan and let sit for 5 minutes. Heat over very low heat until the gelatin is dissolved. Cool slightly. Using an electric mixer, beat the cream and vanilla until soft peaks form. Beat in the lukewarm gelatin very gradually and continue beating until stiff peaks form. Whisk the lemon curd with the lemon juice until smooth. Fold it into the whipped cream, mixing until smooth.

TO ASSEMBLE: Remove the cheesecake from the pan and place on a serving plate. Spread ¾ of the chiffon topping evenly over the cake all the way to the edges. Spoon the remainder of the topping into a piping bag with a large tip and pipe a decorative border around the edge of the cheesecake. Whisk ½ to ¾ cup (120 to 180 mL) of the lemon curd over low heat until it is slightly warm and thin enough to pour. Spoon the lemon curd over the mousse. Tilt the cake to spread the glaze evenly. Chill until set. Store refrigerated in a closed container for up to 4 days.

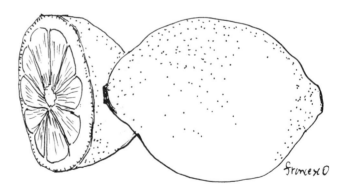

New York–Style Cheesecake

Makes one 10-inch (25-cm) cake (serves 12 to 14)

FOR THE CRUST:

¾ cup (180 mL) cold butter, cut into ½-inch (1.2-cm) pieces

1 ¾ cups (420 mL) all-purpose flour

¼ cup (60 mL) granulated sugar

¼ tsp. (1.2 mL) salt

1 tsp. (5 mL) lemon zest

1 egg, slightly beaten

FOR THE FILLING:

1 ½ lb. (680 g) cream cheese, softened

1 cup (240 mL) sour cream

1 ¼ cups (300 mL) granulated sugar

5 eggs, separated

1 Tbsp. (15 mL) all-purpose flour

1 tsp. (5 mL) vanilla extract

2 tsp. (10 mL) orange zest

1 tsp. (5 mL) lemon zest

2 Tbsp. (30 mL) lemon juice

According to many cheesecake aficionados this classic dessert is the first, best and only cheesecake. A tender but sturdy shortbread crust surrounds the airy filling that gets its lightness from beaten egg whites. You will banish all memories of gloppy, neon-colored fruit topping when you see how easy it is to create your own glistening fruit glaze by simply simmering fresh fruit with a little sugar and cornstarch. That's it, that's all it takes to make the cheesecake of your dreams.

FOR THE CRUST: Using a food processor or pastry cutter, process or cut in the butter with the flour, sugar, salt and zest until mealy. Add the egg and process just until the mixture begins to come together. Divide the dough in half, wrap in plastic and refrigerate for 20 minutes.

Preheat the oven to 375°F (190°C). Roll out one piece of dough into a 10-inch (25-cm) circle. Line the bottom of a springform pan and chill for 20 minutes. Bake for 10 minutes. Cool completely. Roll out the remaining pastry into a strip 3 inches (7.5 cm) wide. Line the sides of the springform pan, overlapping the bottom crust slightly. Trim the pastry just to the top of the pan. Chill while preparing the filling. Reduce the oven setting to 350°F (175°C).

FOR THE FILLING: Using an electric mixer, beat the cream cheese, sour cream and 1 cup (240 mL) of the sugar until light and fluffy, about 5 minutes. Add the egg yolks, flour, vanilla, orange and lemon zests and lemon juice, and beat just until smooth.

Beat the egg whites with the remaining ¼ cup (60 mL) sugar until soft peaks form. Fold into the cheese mixture. Turn into the prepared crust. Bake for 15 minutes, then reduce the oven temperature to 225°F (105°C). Bake for 1 hour and 15 minutes, or until the cake is no longer shiny. Chill for 8 hours or overnight.

FOR THE TOPPING:

½ to 1 cup (120 to 240 mL)
sugar (depending on the
tartness of the fruit)

2 Tbsp. (30 mL) cornstarch

1 Tbsp. (15 mL) lemon juice
(or orange juice for very
tart fruit)

1 tsp. (5 mL) lemon zest (or
orange zest for cranberries)

½ tsp. (2.5 mL) almond
extract (for cherries)

1 lb. (454 g) blueberries, sour
cherries or cranberries

FOR THE TOPPING: Combine the sugar and cornstarch in a medium saucepan. Stir in the juice, zest and almond extract (if using cherries). Mix until smooth, and then stir in the fruit. Cook over low heat, stirring occasionally, until the fruit releases some juice. Increase the temperature to medium and cook, stirring occasionally, until the mixture thickens and begins to boil. Cook for 1 minute, stirring constantly but being careful not to bruise the fruit. Cool slightly before pouring over the chilled cheesecake. Chill thoroughly before removing the cake from the pan. Store refrigerated in a closed container for up to 4 days.

Double Chocolate Truffle Cheesecake

Makes one 10-inch (25-cm) cake (serves 12 to 14)

So much chocolate, so little time. For those of you who don't even glance at dessert unless it has chocolate in it, welcome to chocolate heaven. As if cheesecake isn't rich enough on its own, someone, somewhere, decided it was not and added chocolate to it. If there ever was an example of the success of excess, this is it. Call it overkill, but I call it a good idea.

FOR THE CRUST:

1 ½ cups (360 mL) chocolate wafer crumbs

2 Tbsp. (30 mL) granulated sugar

½ tsp. (2.5 mL) vanilla extract

¼ cup (60 mL) butter, melted

FOR THE FILLING:

1 ½ lb. (680 g) cream cheese, softened

1 ¾ cups (420 mL) granulated sugar

3 eggs

10 oz. (285 g) semisweet chocolate, coarsely chopped

¼ cup (60 mL) whipping cream

1 cup (240 mL) sour cream

⅓ cup (80 mL) coffee liqueur

½ tsp. (2.5 mL) ground cinnamon

1 tsp. (5 mL) vanilla extract

FOR THE GANACHE:

1 cup (240 mL) whipping cream

8 oz. (225 g) semisweet chocolate, coarsely chopped

2 Tbsp. (30 mL) coffee liqueur

2 Tbsp. (30 mL) corn syrup

2 oz. (57 g) milk chocolate, finely chopped

FOR THE CRUST: Preheat the oven to 350°F (175°C). Combine the crumbs, sugar, vanilla and butter in a small bowl, mixing well. Press the mixture into the bottom of a 10-inch (25-cm) springform pan. Bake for 8 minutes. Remove and reduce the oven temperature to 325°F (165°C).

FOR THE FILLING: Using an electric mixer, beat the cream cheese until fluffy, about 5 minutes. Add the sugar and eggs and beat until smooth. Melt the chocolate in a double boiler over hot water or in a microwave. Cool slightly. Add the chocolate, whipping cream and sour cream to the egg mixture and beat until well combined. Stir in the liqueur, cinnamon and vanilla and mix well. Pour the batter into the prepared pan. Bake for 15 minutes and reduce the oven temperature to 225°F (105°C). Bake for 60 to 70 minutes. Cool completely.

FOR THE GANACHE: In a small saucepan or in the microwave, heat the cream until bubbly. Place the chocolate in a medium mixing bowl, pour the cream over top and allow to sit for 2 minutes. Stir until smooth. Add the liqueur and corn syrup and stir to combine. Allow the mixture to cool until slightly thickened. Trim the top of the cake to make it flat. Pour ⅔ of the ganache over the cake, carefully spreading it to the very edge. Chill until set. Spoon the remaining ganache into a pastry bag and pipe a decorative border on the cake. (Warm the ganache slightly, if it's too stiff to pipe.) Melt the milk chocolate in a double boiler over hot water or in the microwave. Using a fork, drizzle it over the top of the cake. Store refrigerated in a closed container up to for 4 days.

VARIATION

CHOCOLATE CHERRY CHEESECAKE: (For those of you who love cherries, read on. To those of you who wouldn't dream of replacing chocolate with anything, my apologies for even suggesting it.) Replace the coffee liqueur with amaretto or cherry liqueur. Take out the cinnamon and add ½ tsp. (2.5 mL) almond extract. For cherry topping, see New York–Style Cheesecake (page 154).

Fresh Peach Melba Cheesecake

Makes one 10-inch (25-cm) cake (serves 12 to 14)

This ethereal, light-as-a-cloud concoction is food for the fairies. The airy whipped filling sits atop a fragile butter crust and is crowned with juicy, brilliant-hued raspberries and peaches, glistening with a tangy fruit glaze.

FOR THE CRUST:

⅔ cup (160 mL) all-purpose flour

2 Tbsp. (30 mL) granulated sugar

pinch salt

¼ cup (60 mL) cold butter, cut into ½-inch (1.2-cm) pieces

1 tsp. (5 mL) lemon zest

2 Tbsp. (30 mL) whipping cream

FOR THE FILLING:

2 envelopes (4½ tsp./22.5 mL) gelatin

3 Tbsp. (45 mL) water

1 cup (240 mL) milk

4 egg yolks

1 cup (240 mL) granulated sugar

1 Tbsp. (15 mL) lemon zest

2 tsp. (10 mL) vanilla extract

1 lb. (454 g) cream cheese, softened

2 cups (475 mL) whipping cream

FOR THE CRUST: Combine the flour, sugar, salt, butter and lemon zest in the bowl of a food processor. Process until mealy. Add the cream and process just until the dough comes together. Press into a disk, wrap in plastic and chill for 20 minutes.

Preheat the oven to 350°F (175°C). Line a baking sheet with parchment paper. On a lightly floured surface, roll the dough out to a 10-inch (25-cm) circle. (Measure generously to allow for shrinkage.) Pierce all over with a fork and chill for 10 minutes. Bake for 12 to 15 minutes, until golden brown. Cool.

FOR THE FILLING: In a small saucepan, combine the gelatin and water. Let sit for 5 minutes.

In a medium saucepan over low heat, heat the milk to just below boiling. Whisk the egg yolks and sugar together. Add ½ cup (120 mL) of the hot milk, whisking until smooth. Add the egg mixture to the milk in the saucepan, whisking until smooth. Cook over medium-low heat, stirring constantly with a wooden spoon, until the mixture thickens and begins to bubble, about 8 to 10 minutes. Remove from the heat, stir in the zest, vanilla and dissolved gelatin. Pour into a large bowl and cool.

Using an electric mixer, whip the cream cheese until smooth. Add to the cooled custard, beating thoroughly. Whip the cream with an electric mixer until stiff peaks form. Fold into the cream cheese mixture.

Line the side of a 10-inch (25-cm) springform pan with a strip of parchment paper. Place the cooled crust in the prepared cake pan. Spread the cream cheese mixture over the crust. Chill until set.

FOR THE TOPPING:

2 to 3 ripe, firm peaches

2 cups (475 mL) raspberries

¾ cup (180 mL) raspberry
   or apricot jam, or red
   currant jelly

2 Tbsp. (30 mL) framboise or
   Grand Marnier

1 cup (240 mL) unblanched
   sliced almonds, toasted

FOR THE TOPPING: Cover the peaches with boiling water for 60 seconds. Drain, and when they are cool enough to handle, peel them and cut them in half, removing the pit. Slice into ¼-inch (.6-cm) slices. Place them on the surface of the chilled cheesecake, overlapping the slices in a decorative design and leaving room at the edge of the cake for the raspberries. Surround the peach slices with raspberries.

Melt the jam or jelly with the liqueur in a small saucepan over low heat. Cook for about 5 minutes to reduce by about ⅓. Brush the raspberries and peaches with the glaze and drizzle any remaining glaze in the spaces between the fruit. Refrigerate until set. Remove the cheesecake from the pan and peel away the parchment paper. Press the toasted almonds into the sides of the cake. Place on a serving plate and refrigerate until serving time. Store refrigerated in a tightly closed container for up to 4 days.

Pumpkin Cheesecake

Makes one 10-inch (25-cm) cake (serves 12 to 14)

FOR THE CRUST:

2 cups (475 mL) gingersnap
cookie crumbs

3 Tbsp. (45 mL) granulated
sugar

¼ tsp. (1.2 mL) ground
cinnamon

⅓ cup (80 mL) butter, melted
and hot

FOR THE FILLING:

1½ lb. (680 g) cream cheese,
softened

½ cup (120 mL) granulated
sugar

½ cup (120 mL) brown sugar

¾ cup (180 mL) whipping
cream

1 cup (240 mL) pumpkin
purée

5 eggs

2 Tbsp. (30 mL) all-purpose
flour

1 tsp. (5 mL) ground
cinnamon

½ tsp. (2.5 mL) ground
nutmeg

½ tsp. (2.5 mL) ground ginger

½ tsp. (2.5 mL) ground cloves

¼ tsp. (1.2 mL) salt

I'm not entirely convinced of this combination, but the votes are in; there are enough fans out there to twist my arm sufficiently to include this recipe. What pumpkin pie lovers find most appealing about their favorite pie is exactly what makes pumpkin cheesecake so delicious: creamy, dreamy smoothness and richness of texture that is even more pronounced with the addition of softened whipped cream cheese. Maybe you can do without the candied ginger and toasted pecans, but don't even think about skipping the whipped cream—it's mandatory.

FOR THE CRUST: Preheat the oven to 350°F (175°C). Combine the cookie crumbs, sugar, cinnamon and melted butter in a small bowl, mixing well. Press into the bottom and sides of a 10-inch (25-cm) springform pan. Bake for 8 minutes.

FOR THE FILLING: Using an electric mixer, beat the cream cheese, both sugars and cream until light and fluffy, about 8 minutes. Beat in the pumpkin. Add the remaining filling ingredients and beat just until combined. Pour the batter into the prepared crust. Bake for 15 minutes and then reduce the temperature to 225°F (105°C). Bake for 1 hour and 10 minutes, or until the center is set and the surface is no longer shiny. Chill for 8 hours or overnight. Remove from the pan and place on a serving plate.

FOR THE TOPPING:

1½ cups (360 mL) whipping cream

2 Tbsp. (30 mL) granulated sugar

1 tsp. (5 mL) vanilla extract

⅓ cup (80 mL) candied ginger, finely chopped

⅓ cup (80 L) toasted pecans, coarsely chopped

FOR THE TOPPING: Using an electric mixer, whip the cream, sugar and vanilla until stiff peaks form. Pipe onto the chilled whole cheesecake or on each individual serving. Sprinkle with the candied ginger and pecans. Store refrigerated in a closed container for up to 4 days.

Amaretto Cheesecake

Makes one 10-inch (25-cm) cake (serves 12 to 16)

FOR THE CRUST:

1 cup (240 mL) amaretti cookie crumbs (if unavailable use vanilla wafers and ¼ tsp./1.2 mL almond extract)

¾ cup (180 mL) toasted blanched almonds, very finely chopped

¼ cup (60 mL) butter, melted and hot

FOR THE FILLING:

1 envelope (2¼ tsp./11 mL) gelatin

2 Tbsp. (30 mL) water

1 cup (240 mL) half-and-half

3 eggs, separated

1 cup (240 mL) granulated sugar

1¼ lb. (565 g) cream cheese, softened

½ cup (120 mL) amaretto

½ tsp. (2.5 mL) almond extract

1¼ cups (300 mL) whipping cream

¼ cup (60 mL) granulated sugar

pinch salt

A sublime, understated cloud of a cheesecake, almond-scented and topped with delicate sugar-encrusted almonds. Very elegant, very adult and very yummy.

FOR THE CRUST: Preheat the oven to 325°F (165°C). Combine the crust ingredients in a small bowl, mixing well. Press into the bottom of a 10-inch (25-cm) springform pan. Bake for 10 minutes. Cool.

FOR THE FILLING: Sprinkle the gelatin over the water in a small saucepan. Let sit for 5 minutes. Heat over low heat until warm; do not boil. Stir until dissolved. In a medium saucepan over low heat, heat the half-and-half to just below boiling. Beat the egg yolks with the 1 cup (240 mL) sugar until pale and fluffy, about 5 to 6 minutes. Add ½ cup (120 mL) of the hot cream to the eggs, whisking until smooth. Add the egg yolk mixture to the cream in the saucepan, whisking until smooth. Cook over medium-low heat, stirring constantly with a wooden spoon, until the mixture thickens and begins to bubble, about 3 to 5 minutes. Remove from the heat and stir in the gelatin. Cool slightly for about 15 to 20 minutes.

Using an electric mixer, beat the cream cheese until smooth. Mix in the amaretto and almond extract. Add the warm egg yolk mixture gradually, combining thoroughly. Cool completely in the refrigerator, stirring occasionally.

Using an electric mixer, whip the whipping cream until stiff peaks form. Clean the beaters and beat the egg whites until soft peaks form. Add the ¼ cup (60 mL) sugar and the salt and beat until the mixture forms peaks but is not dry. Fold the beaten egg whites into the cooled cream cheese mixture and then fold in the whipped cream. Pour over the cooled crust. Refrigerate at least 3 to 4 hours.

Preheat the oven to 350°F (175°C). Line a cookie sheet with parchment paper.

1 large egg white, room
temperature

1 ¼ cups (300 mL) sliced
blanched almonds

2 Tbsp. (30 mL) granulated
sugar

¾ cup (180 mL) whipping
cream

3 Tbsp. (45 mL) icing sugar

2 Tbsp. (30 mL) amaretto

FOR THE TOPPING: Whisk the egg white until foamy. Stir in the almonds until they are evenly coated. Sprinkle the granulated sugar over the nuts and stir to combine. Spread in a single layer on the cookie sheet. Bake until golden, about 10 to 15 minutes, stirring occasionally. Remove and loosen the nuts. Cool.

Using an electric mixer, whip the cream with the icing sugar and amaretto until stiff. Pipe over the chilled cake and decorate with the toasted almonds. Store refrigerated in a tightly closed container for up to 4 days.

Layer Cakes and Tortes

Whether it is the simplest dark fudge layer cake or an extravagant flourless meringue torte, no one is immune to the seduction of a beautifully presented cake. While other desserts can be eaten every day, layer cakes are usually reserved for those extra-special occasions, such as birthdays, weddings and anniversaries.

In this chapter, the delicious array of desserts includes unadorned, straightforward recipes that can be whipped up easily, as well as slightly more demanding creations that will ensure a dazzling finale for the most festive of occasions.

Double Dutch Chocolate Cake

Makes one 10-inch (25-cm) layer cake (serves 12 to 14)

FOR THE CAKE:

¾ cup (180 mL) oil

3 eggs

2 cups (475 mL) brown sugar

1 cup (240 mL) granulated sugar

1½ cups (360 mL) buttermilk

1¼ cups (300 mL) cocoa, preferably Dutch-process

2 tsp. (10 mL) vanilla extract

2⅔ cup (640 mL) all-purpose flour

2 tsp. (10 mL) baking soda

¾ tsp. (4 mL) baking powder

½ tsp. (2.5 mL) salt

1½ cups (360 mL) hot brewed coffee

FOR THE FROSTING:

3 cups (720 mL) whipping cream

½ cup (120 mL) butter

¼ cup (60 mL) granulated sugar

2 lb. (900 g) semisweet chocolate, finely chopped

1 tsp. (5 mL) vanilla extract

When I hear the words "chocolate cake" it is not some elaborate, exotically layered concoction involving genoises, ganaches, sabayon, marjolaines and so on that springs to mind. It it old-fashioned classic chocolate cake—multi-layered, stick-to-the-fork moist and smothered in thick swirls of dark chocolate frosting. I actually spent more time on research and development for this cake than I did on many of the more elaborate recipes. After many experiments, I am satisfied with the final result—a cake that is dense but not heavy; dark and intense but still sweet enough to satisfy even young children; and moist and light with a tender, delicate crumble. And that was just the cake; then there was the all-important frosting! What worked best to produce a dark, creamy, intensely chocolatey icing was a simple combination of semisweet chocolate, cream and butter. Don't be alarmed at the amount of chocolate in the frosting recipe. One bite of this cake and you'll agree it's not one ounce too much!

FOR THE CAKE: Preheat the oven to 325°F (165°C). Lightly butter three 10-inch (25-cm) cake pans and line them with parchment paper.

Using an electric mixer, beat the oil, eggs, both sugars, buttermilk, cocoa and vanilla for 2 or 3 minutes. In a separate bowl, sift the flour, baking soda, baking powder and salt. Add to the cocoa mixture and beat until smooth. Pour in the hot coffee and mix until thoroughly combined. Pour the batter into the prepared pans and bake for 25 to 30 minutes, until a cake tester inserted in the center of the cake comes out clean. Cool completely in the pans.

FOR THE FROSTING: In a medium saucepan over low heat or in the microwave, heat the cream, butter and sugar, stirring occasionally, until the sugar dissolves completely and the mixture comes to a simmer. Place the chopped chocolate in a medium bowl, add the cream mixture and let sit for 5 minutes. Stir to

FOR THE GLAZE:

¾ cup (180 mL) whipping cream

6 oz. (180 g) semisweet chocolate, finely chopped

1 Tbsp. (15 mL) corn syrup

2 Tbsp. (30 mL) rum or brandy (optional)

chocolate curls (optional)

melt the chocolate completely, then add the vanilla. Cool for 1 to 2 hours, stirring occasionally, until the frosting is of spreading consistency.

Remove the parchment paper from the cake layers. Place one layer on a serving plate. Cover with ¼ of the frosting. Top with the second layer and ¼ of the frosting. Place the third layer on top. Frost the sides and then the top of the cake with the remaining frosting. Smooth with a metal spatula dipped in hot water.

FOR THE GLAZE: In a small saucepan over low heat or in the microwave, heat the cream to a slow simmer. Place the chopped chocolate in a small bowl, add the hot cream and let sit for 5 minutes. Stir to melt the chocolate completely, and then stir in the corn syrup and rum or brandy. Cool until slightly thickened but still very shiny.

Reserve ½ cup (120 mL) of the glaze and refrigerate. Warm the remaining glaze slightly, if necessary, to pouring consistency by heating gently over low heat or in the microwave in 5- to 10-second intervals. Pour the glaze over the cake, smoothing in a circular motion with a long metal spatula, and allowing the glaze to drizzle decoratively down the sides of the cake. Chill to set, and then pipe rosettes on the top of the cake with the remaining glaze. Decorate the top of the cake with chocolate curls, if desired. (For an easier, more casual look, omit the glaze and chocolate curls. Swirl and peak the frosting on the cake with a spatula.)

Serve at room temperature. Store at room temperature in a closed container for up to 3 days, refrigerated for up to 6 days.

German Chocolate Cake

Makes one 10-inch (25-cm) layer cake (serves 12 to 14)

FOR THE CAKE:

¾ cup (180 mL) oil

3 eggs

3 cups (720 mL) granulated sugar

1½ cups (360 mL) buttermilk

1 cup (240 mL) cocoa, preferably Dutch-process

2 tsp. (10 mL) vanilla extract

2⅔ cups (640 mL) all-purpose flour

2 tsp. (10 mL) baking soda

¾ tsp. (4 mL) baking powder

½ tsp. (2.5 mL) salt

1½ cups (360 mL) hot water

FOR THE FROSTING:

1 cup (240 mL) icing sugar

2 Tbsp. (30 mL) cornstarch

2 cups (475 mL) whipping cream, scalded

2½ cups (600 mL) sweetened shredded coconut

1½ cups (360 mL) coarsely chopped pecans

1 tsp. (5 mL) vanilla extract

12 pecan halves

A familiar sight in many traditional cookbooks, this classic gets its name from the original use of "German" chocolate, a brand of sweet milk chocolate. Although I've taken the liberty of making a dark chocolate cake, which I feel is a better counterpoint to the sweetness of the filling, the gooey pecan and coconut frosting is in keeping with the spirit of the original. This is a sweet, delectably moist and very satisfying cake.

FOR THE CAKE: Preheat the oven to 325°F (165°C). Lightly butter three 10-inch (25-cm) cake pans and line the bottoms with parchment paper.

Using an electric mixer, beat the oil, eggs, sugar, buttermilk, cocoa and vanilla for 2 to 3 minutes. In a separate bowl, sift the flour with the baking soda, baking powder and salt, and add to the cocoa mixture. Add the hot water and mix until thoroughly combined. Pour into the prepared cake pans and bake for 25 minutes, or until a cake tester inserted in the center of the cake comes out clean. Cool completely in the pans before assembly.

FOR THE FROSTING: Mix the sugar and cornstarch in a medium saucepan. Stir in the hot cream. Cook over low heat, stirring constantly, until bubbling and thickened, about 5 minutes. Stir in the coconut, chopped pecans and vanilla. Cover and cool to room temperature.

Loosen the sides of the cakes and remove from the pans. Peel off the parchment paper. Place one cake layer on a serving plate. Spread ¼ of the frosting over the cake. Cover with the second layer and spread with ¼ of the frosting. Repeat with the third layer and use the remaining ¼ of the frosting to frost the sides. Decorate with the pecan halves. Store refrigerated in a closed container for up to 5 days.

Chocolate Caramel Mousse Cake

Makes one 10-inch (25-cm) cake (serves 12 to 14)

FOR THE GENOISE:

½ cup (120 mL) all-purpose flour

½ cup (120 mL) cocoa, preferably Dutch-process

1 tsp. (5 mL) baking powder

¼ tsp. (1.2 mL) salt

6 eggs at room temperature, separated

1 cup (240 mL) granulated sugar

1 tsp. (5 mL) vanilla extract

½ cup (120 mL) butter, melted and cooled

FOR THE CARAMEL:

1½ cups (360 mL) granulated sugar

½ cup (120 mL) water

2 Tbsp. (30 mL) corn syrup

½ cup (120 mL) whipping cream

¼ cup (60 mL) butter, cut into ½-inch (1.2-cm) pieces

1 tsp. (5 mL) vanilla extract

½ cup (120 mL) diced blanched almonds, lightly toasted

Many chocolate desserts lack discretion; they are over the top, disgustingly gooey and proud of it. This is not one of them. That's not to say this cake isn't extraordinarily rich and chocolatey; the delectable, moist, genoise layers sandwich a dreamy bittersweet mousse that sits atop buttery caramel and toasted almonds. But the sleek ganache coating and minimalist decorations make for an understated, elegant presentation that belies the indulgence within.

FOR THE GENOISE: Preheat the oven to 350°F (175°C). Butter a 10-inch (25-cm) cake pan and line the bottom with parchment paper.

Sift the flour, cocoa, baking powder and salt together. Using an electric mixer at high speed, beat the egg yolks with ½ cup (120 mL) of the sugar and the vanilla until light and doubled in volume, about 5 minutes. In a separate bowl, using clean beaters, beat the egg whites until soft peaks form. Continue beating, gradually adding the remaining ½ cup (120 mL) of sugar to the egg whites. Beat until stiff but not dry, about 2 minutes. Fold the egg whites into the yolks, combining them carefully. Sift the flour mixture over the egg mixture and fold it in. Remove 1 cup (240 mL) of the batter and mix it into the melted butter. Return the mixture to the remaining batter and fold it in carefully but thoroughly. Spread in the prepared pan. Bake for 15 to 20 minutes, or until a cake tester inserted in the center of the cake comes out clean. Cool completely in the pan. Remove from the pan, peel off the parchment paper and split into 2 layers. Place one layer on the bottom of a 10-inch (25-cm) springform pan.

FOR THE CARAMEL: Bring the sugar, water and syrup to a boil in a heavy saucepan over medium heat, stirring constantly. When the mixture begins to boil, stop stirring and cook to a medium golden color, about 8 minutes. Remove from the heat and, stirring carefully, add the cream slowly. Add the butter

FOR THE MOUSSE:

10 oz. (285 g) semisweet
   chocolate, coarsely chopped

¼ cup (60 mL) butter

4 eggs at room temperature,
   separated

¼ cup (60 mL) sugar

1 cup (240 mL) whipping
   cream

FOR THE GANACHE:

1 cup (240 mL) whipping
   cream

8 oz. (225 g) semisweet
   chocolate, coarsely chopped

2 Tbsp. (30 mL) corn syrup

2 Tbsp. (30 mL) brandy

and vanilla and stir to combine. Drizzle ½ the warm caramel over the cake layer in the springform pan. Sprinkle with the almonds.

FOR THE MOUSSE: In a medium saucepan over low heat, or in the microwave, heat the chocolate and butter, stirring until melted. Cool to lukewarm. Mix the egg yolks and sugar in a large bowl. Using an electric mixer, whip the cream until it's almost stiff. In a separate bowl, using clean beaters, beat the whites until soft peaks form. Do not overbeat. Combine the cooled chocolate and the egg yolks. Fold in the whipped cream and then the beaten egg whites, mixing until just combined. Spread the mousse over the caramel and almonds. Cover with the remaining cake layer. Press firmly to make a level surface. Chill until firm, 4 to 6 hours.

FOR THE GANACHE: In a small saucepan over low heat or in the microwave, heat the cream to a slow simmer. Remove from the heat and stir in the chocolate. Let sit for 5 minutes. Stir to melt the chocolate completely, and then stir in the corn syrup and brandy. Cool until slightly thickened but still shiny.

Remove the cake from the springform pan and invert it onto a wire rack. Place a larger plate below the rack. Pour the ganache over the cake, covering the top and sides, using a long metal spatula to spread and smooth the ganache. If the ganache layer is too thin, chill the glazed cake, then repeat the procedure. Warm the glaze slightly, if necessary, until it is the right consistency for pouring.

Using a wide spatula, transfer the cake to a serving plate. In a small saucepan over low heat, or in the microwave, heat the remaining caramel until it is thin enough to pour. Place it in a pastry bag with a very small tip. Decorate the top of the cake by piping a fine grid ¾ inch (2 cm) apart over the surface of the ganache. Store refrigerated in a closed container for up to 4 days.

Chocolate Apricot Truffle Torte

Makes one 10-inch (25-cm) cake (serves 12 to 14)

FOR THE CAKE:

⅔ cup (160 mL) dried apricots, coarsely chopped

½ cup (120 mL) brandy

1 lb. (455 g) semisweet chocolate, coarsely chopped

1 cup (240 mL) butter

½ cup (120 mL) strong coffee, at room temperature

7 eggs, separated

1 cup (240 mL) sugar

1 tsp. (5 mL) vanilla extract

½ cup (120 mL) pastry flour

1¼ cups (300 mL) toasted hazelnuts, finely ground

⅓ cup (80 mL) granulated sugar

FOR THE GLAZE:

1 cup (240 mL) whipping cream

10 oz. (285 g) semisweet chocolate, coarsely chopped

1 Tbsp. (15 mL) corn syrup

1 Tbsp. (15 mL) brandy

With its sleek, glistening exterior and dark-as-midnight filling, this cake looks sinful enough, but take one bite and you'll realize this is not merely indulgence, it is pure seduction. Vary the type of nuts, liqueurs and dried fruit for a variety of flavors. Try dried cherries with almonds and amaretto, or, for a fruity exotic combination, candied ginger, macadamias and rum. Best prepared a day in advance; this cake actually improves in flavor if wrapped unglazed and stored in the refrigerator for up to two weeks. Glaze it the day you serve it.

FOR THE CAKE: Soak the apricots in the brandy for 2 hours. Preheat the oven to 325°F (165°C). Butter a 10-inch (25-cm) springform pan, line it with parchment paper, and butter and flour the paper.

Melt the chocolate with the butter and coffee over low heat in a medium saucepan or in the microwave. Cool. Using an electric mixer, beat the egg yolks with the 1 cup (240 mL) sugar and vanilla until light and thick, about 5 minutes. Add the cooled chocolate and stir to combine. Add the flour and ground hazelnuts and fold into the mixture. Gently stir in the apricots, with the brandy.

Using an electric mixer with clean beaters, beat the egg whites until soft peaks form. Add the ⅓ cup (80 mL) sugar a little at a time and beat until it forms firm peaks but is still soft and shiny. Fold the egg whites carefully into the chocolate mixture, so as to not deflate the whites. Spread the batter in the prepared pan. Bake for 45 minutes. Do not test for doneness, as the cake will be very moist. Cool the cake completely in the pan.

FOR THE GLAZE: In a medium saucepan over low heat, or in the microwave, heat the cream to a slow simmer. Remove from the heat and stir in the chocolate. Let sit for 5 minutes. Stir to melt the chocolate completely, and then stir in the corn syrup and brandy. Cool until slightly thickened but still very shiny.

TO ASSEMBLE:

2 oz. (57 g) white chocolate, finely chopped

chocolate curls, for garnish

TO ASSEMBLE: Remove the cake from the pan and invert it onto a wire rack. Place a larger plate below the rack. Pour the glaze over the cake, smoothing it with a long metal spatula and letting the excess flow over the side and onto the plate underneath. Transfer the cake with a long, wide metal spatula to a serving plate. In a double boiler over hot water or in the microwave, melt the white chocolate. Drizzle the chocolate decoratively over the top of the cake and top with chocolate curls. Store refrigerated in a closed container for up to 7 days.

Chocolate Hazelnut Torte

Makes one 10-inch (25-cm) layer cake (serves 12 to 14)

FOR THE CAKE:

2 cups (475 mL) toasted hazelnuts

2 Tbsp. (30 mL) all-purpose flour

⅔ cup (160 mL) granulated sugar

7 egg whites, room temperature

¼ tsp. (60 mL) cream of tartar

⅓ cup (80 mL) granulated sugar

FOR THE BUTTERCREAM:

½ cup (120 mL) water

1 cup (240 mL) granulated sugar

1 egg

2 egg yolks

1½ cups (360 mL) butter, softened

¾ cup (180 mL) Praline, made with hazelnuts (see page 208)

12 oz. (360 g) semisweet chocolate, coarsely chopped

2 Tbsp. (30 mL) Frangelico

¼ cup (60 mL) water

Don't be alarmed by the seemingly endless number of steps in this European-style classic, it is actually not that difficult and the task will seem less daunting if you familiarize yourself with each procedure before beginning. It is well worth the effort, resulting in a gorgeous, sophisticated jewel of a cake, a dazzling layered masterpiece that serves beautifully and never fails to impress. This cake is best made at least a day in advance, to allow the flavors to mellow. Store it covered in the refrigerator, but be sure to serve it at room temperature for optimum taste and texture.

FOR THE CAKE: Preheat the oven to 325°F (165°C). Lightly butter four 10-inch (25-cm) cake pans and line the bottoms with parchment paper.

Using a food processor, grind the hazelnuts and flour until mealy. Add the ⅔ cup (160 mL) sugar and process until powdery. Using an electric mixer, beat the egg whites and cream of tartar until frothy. Gradually beat in ⅓ cup (80 mL) sugar until stiff but not dry. Fold the nut mixture into the egg whites, being careful not to deflate the mixture. Spread the batter evenly in the prepared pans. Bake for 25 to 30 minutes, or until the top is golden and the cake springs back when lightly pressed. Cool completely in the pans before assembly.

FOR THE BUTTERCREAM: In a medium saucepan combine the water and sugar. Cover and bring to a simmer over medium heat. Cook covered until the sugar dissolves completely, about 2 minutes. Uncover and cook without stirring until the syrup almost reaches the hard-ball stage. (Drop a small amount in very cold water; at the hard-ball stage, a very firm but still pliable ball is produced.)

While the mixture is cooking, beat the egg and egg yolks in a large bowl with an electric mixer until the eggs are pale and thick, about 5 to 7 minutes. When the syrup reaches the right temperature, reduce the speed of the mixer and pour the hot

1 cup (240 mL) toasted hazelnuts, coarsely chopped
½ cup (120 mL) Praline,
   made with hazelnuts
   (see page 208)

syrup in a very thin stream over the beaten eggs, avoiding the beaters and the sides of the bowl (the syrup will harden quickly if not poured directly onto the eggs). Continue beating until the mixture reaches room temperature. Add the butter, 2 table-spoons (30 mL) at a time, beating just until the mixture is soft and creamy.

Remove 1½ cups (360 mL) of the buttercream. Using a food processor, finely grind the hazelnut praline until powdery. Combine with the reserved 1½ cups (360 mL) buttercream and set aside.

In a small saucepan over low heat or in the microwave, heat the chocolate, liqueur and water. Stir until smooth. Cool to lukewarm, then combine with the remaining buttercream. Do not beat. Set aside.

TO ASSEMBLE: Loosen the sides of the cakes and remove them from the pans. Peel off the parchment paper. Place one cake on a serving plate. Spread with ½ of the hazelnut buttercream and top with a second cake. Spread with ¾ cup (180 mL) of the chocolate buttercream and top with the third cake. Spread with the remaining hazelnut buttercream and top with the fourth cake. Chill for 20 to 30 minutes.

Spread the top and sides of the cake with the chocolate buttercream, reserving ½ cup (120 mL) for decoration. Press the chopped hazelnuts into the sides of the cake. Spoon the remaining buttercream into a piping bag with a star tip and pipe a decorative edge around the cake. Decorate with the praline pieces.

Mocha Walnut Torte

Makes one 10-inch (25-cm) layer cake (serves 12 to 14)

FOR THE CAKE:

8 eggs, room temperature, separated

⅔ cup (160 mL) granulated sugar

1⅔ cups (400 mL) walnuts

2 Tbsp. (30 mL) granulated sugar

2 Tbsp. (300 mL) bread-crumbs

1½ Tbsp. (22.5 mL) strong coffee

1½ Tbsp. (22.5 mL) rum

1 tsp. (5 mL) vanilla extract

¼ tsp. (1.2 mL) salt

2 Tbsp. (30 mL) granulated sugar

FOR THE FILLING:

1⅔ cups (400 mL) walnuts

¼ cup (60 mL) granulated sugar

⅓ cup (80 mL) milk

¾ cup (180 mL) granulated sugar

¾ cup (180 mL) butter, softened

½ tsp. (2.5 mL) vanilla extract

My earliest and most vivid memory of any dessert is my mother's traditional Polish walnut torte at Christmas. I have taken very few liberties with my mother's recipe. It is an incredibly rich flourless cake, with no additional leavening beyond the beaten egg whites. The layers bake up tender and moist with a very pronounced walnut flavor that is repeated in the creamy filling. The crowning glory of this very European torte is the unbelievably buttery, bittersweet mocha buttercream. This is a special-occasion dessert best served in small wedges at room temperature, although I clearly recall that my brother and I had no problem consuming giant slices straight out of the refrigerator late at night, in our pajamas by the Christmas tree.

FOR THE CAKE: Preheat the oven to 325°F (165°C). Lightly butter three 10-inch (25-cm) cake pans and line the bottoms with parchment paper.

Using an electric mixer, beat the egg yolks and the ⅔ cup (160 mL) sugar until light and fluffy, about 5 minutes. Using a food processor, grind the nuts and 2 Tbsp. (30 mL) of sugar until powdery. Add the nuts, breadcrumbs, coffee, rum and vanilla to the beaten egg yolks and stir to combine. Set aside.

Using a clean bowl and beaters, beat the egg whites and salt until frothy. Gradually add the remaining 2 Tbsp. (30 mL) sugar and beat until stiff peaks form. Fold about ¼ of the egg white mixture into the batter, and then gently fold in the remainder. Spread evenly in the prepared pans. Bake for 30 to 35 minutes, or until the cake springs back when lightly pressed. Cool completely in the pans before assembly.

FOR THE FILLING: Using a food processor, grind the walnuts and the ¼ cup (60 mL) sugar until powdery. Combine the milk and the ¾ cup (180 mL) sugar in a medium saucepan. Bring to a boil over medium heat, stirring constantly. Remove from the heat and stir in the ground walnuts. Cool. Using a wooden spoon, beat in the butter and vanilla until light and fluffy.

FOR THE BUTTERCREAM:

1 ¼ cups (300 mL) granulated
sugar

¾ cup (180 mL) water

¾ cup (180 mL) egg yolks
(approximately 4 or 5 yolks)

1 ½ Tbsp. (22.5 mL) instant
coffee powder

2 ½ cups (600 mL) butter,
softened

1 Tbsp. (15 mL) chopped
semisweet chocolate, melted

2 tsp. (10 mL) vanilla extract

TO ASSEMBLE:

1 cup (240 mL) finely
chopped walnuts

12 walnut halves

FOR THE BUTTERCREAM: In a medium saucepan, combine the sugar and water. Cook over medium heat without stirring, swirling the pan to mix the sugar as it caramelizes. Cook until the mixture is dark golden and syrupy, about 8 to 10 minutes. Remove from the heat promptly to prevent scorching. Cool the caramel until it is just warm. Whisk the egg yolks with the instant coffee. Add to the warm caramel and return to the heat. Cook over low heat, whisking constantly, until it is just beginning to bubble. Do not boil. Remove from the heat.

Using an electric mixer, beat the mixture until it is light and fluffy and has cooled. Beat in the soft butter, melted chocolate and vanilla until creamy and light.

TO ASSEMBLE: Loosen the sides of the cakes and remove them from the pans. Peel off the parchment paper. Cut each cake in half horizontally, using a long serrated knife. Place one half on a serving plate and spread with ⅕ of the filling. Repeat with the other 5 layers, ending with the final cake layer.

Reserve ½ cup (120 mL) of the buttercream. Spread the remaining buttercream over the top and sides of the cake. Spoon the reserved buttercream into a piping bag with a star tip and pipe 12 rosettes around the edge of the cake. Press the chopped walnuts into the sides of the cake. Decorate the top with the 12 walnut halves. Store in a closed container at room temperature for up to 3 days, refrigerated for up to 6 days.

Strawberry Mocha Meringue Torte

Makes one 10-inch (25-cm) layer cake (serves 12 to 14)

FOR THE CAKE:

¾ cup (180 mL) butter, softened

⅓ cup (80 mL) granulated sugar

½ cup (120 mL) brown sugar

6 egg yolks

1 tsp. (5 mL) vanilla extract

⅓ cup (80 mL) cocoa powder, preferably Dutch-process

½ cup (120 mL) hot water

1½ cups (360 mL) all-purpose flour

1½ tsp. (7.5 mL) baking powder

½ tsp. (2.5 mL) baking soda

¼ tsp. (1.2 mL) salt

FOR THE MERINGUE:

6 egg whites, room temperature

1¼ cups (300 mL) granulated sugar

½ tsp (2.5 mL) almond extract

½ cup (120 mL) ground almonds

¾ cup (180 mL) sliced blanched almonds

This is for those occasions when you want to present something that makes you feel like you've outdone yourself. Sometimes it's all about showing off. Yes, it's okay to bask in the adulation of your eagerly waiting guests. This cake, with its delicate, moist chocolate layer, fragile meringue and opulent mocha mousse crowned with strawberries, is a tour de force you will be thrilled to serve.

FOR THE CAKE: Preheat the oven to 350°F (175°C). Butter three 10-inch (25-cm) cake pans and line the bottoms with parchment paper.

Using an electric mixer, beat the butter and both sugars until light and fluffy. Add the egg yolks one at a time, beating well after each addition. Beat in the vanilla. Whisk the cocoa and hot water together in a small bowl. Sift the flour, baking powder, baking soda and salt in a separate bowl. Add the dry ingredients to the butter mixture in 3 parts, alternating with the cocoa mixture. Mix just until combined. Spread the batter evenly in the prepared pans. Set aside and prepare the meringue layer.

FOR THE MERINGUE: Using an electric mixer, beat the egg whites until soft peaks form. Gradually add the sugar, beating until the meringue is very stiff and glossy. Stir in the almond extract. Fold in the ground almonds. Spread the meringue evenly over the cake batter in the pans. Sprinkle with the almonds. Bake for 25 to 30 minutes, until golden. Cool completely in the pans before assembling.

FOR THE MOUSSE:

3 cups (720 mL) whipping
  cream

2 Tbsp. (30 mL) instant coffee
  granules

3 oz. (85 g) semisweet chocolate, finely chopped

¼ cup (60 mL) icing sugar

2 Tbsp. (30 mL) coffee liqueur

TO ASSEMBLE:

4 oz. (113 g) semisweet
  chocolate, finely chopped

12 strawberries

FOR THE MOUSSE: In a small saucepan over medium heat or in the microwave, heat 1 cup (240 mL) of the cream with the instant coffee until the mixture just begins to boil. Add the chocolate and let sit for 5 minutes. Stir until the chocolate has melted. Transfer to a medium metal bowl and chill until cool, stirring occasionally.

Combine the remaining 2 cups (475 mL) of cream with the cooled chocolate mixture, icing sugar and coffee liqueur. Whip until stiff peaks form.

TO ASSEMBLE: Loosen the sides of the cakes and remove them from the pans. Peel off the parchment paper. Place one cake on a serving plate. Set aside ¼ of the mousse. Pipe or spread ½ of the remaining mousse onto the first cake layer, making sure the mousse comes just to the edge of the cake. Top with the second layer. Repeat the mousse layer and top with the remaining cake layer. Spoon the reserved mousse into a piping bag with a star tip and pipe 12 large rosettes around the outside of the cake.

Melt the chocolate in a double boiler over hot water or in the microwave. Using a fork, drizzle ¼ of the chocolate over the cake. Dip the strawberries halfway in the remaining choco-late and set onto the rosettes. Store refrigerated in a closed container for up to 3 days.

Lemon Meringue Cake

Makes one 10-inch (25-cm) cake (serves 12 to 14)

FOR THE CAKE:

1 cup (240 mL) granulated
  sugar

2 eggs

½ cup (120 mL) oil

⅓ cup (80 mL) orange juice

2 Tbsp. (30 mL) lemon juice

1 tsp. (5 mL) lemon zest

½ tsp. (2.5 mL) vanilla
  extract

1 ¼ cups (300 mL) all-purpose
  flour

1 tsp. (5 mL) baking powder

pinch salt

FOR THE MERINGUE:

6 egg whites, room tem-
  perature

¼ tsp. (1.2 mL) cream of tartar

1 ¼ cups (300 mL) granulated
  sugar

¼ tsp. (1.2 mL) almond
  extract

2 cups (475 mL) sliced
  blanched almonds

Inspired by the very popular classic pie of the same name, this pretty, delightfully light cake makes a perfect ending for a summer barbecue or picnic. The crispy almond meringue, layered with clouds of lemon mousse, softens and takes on a wonderfully tender texture.

FOR THE CAKE: Preheat the oven to 350°F (175°C). Butter one 10-inch (25-cm) round cake pan and line it with parchment paper.

Using an electric mixer, beat the sugar and eggs until light. Beat in the oil, orange and lemon juice, lemon zest and vanilla. Sift the flour, baking powder and salt together and add to the egg mixture. Beat until well combined. Pour into the prepared pan. Bake for 20 to 30 minutes, or until a cake tester inserted in the center of the cake comes out clean. Cool completely in the pan before assembly.

FOR THE MERINGUE: Reduce the oven temperature to 325°F (165°C). Cut two 10-inch (25-cm) circles from parchment paper. Trace 9½-inch (24-cm) circles on the parchment. Turn upside down to prevent the ink from transferring to the meringue. Place the parchment circles on baking sheets. Using an electric mixer, beat the egg whites and cream of tartar until soft peaks form. Gradually add the sugar, beating until the meringue is very stiff and glossy. Stir in the almond extract and then fold the almonds into the meringue. Divide the meringue between the two parchment circles, spreading it evenly to 9½ inches (24 cm) and keeping the edges round and neat (the meringue will spread slightly to 10 inches/25 cm). Bake for 50 to 60 minutes until the meringues are pale golden and almost firm. Cool completely before assembling the cake.

FOR THE MOUSSE:

1 envelope (2 $\frac{1}{4}$ tsp./11 mL)
   gelatin

1 Tbsp. (15 mL) water

1 Tbsp. (15 mL) lemon juice

3 cups (720 mL) whipping
   cream

1 tsp. (5 mL) vanilla extract

1 $\frac{1}{2}$ cups (360 mL) Lemon
   Curd (see page 216)

TO ASSEMBLE:

$\frac{1}{2}$ cup (120 mL) almonds,
   toasted and sliced

FOR THE MOUSSE: In a small saucepan, combine the gelatin and water and let sit for 5 minutes. Heat over very low heat, until the gelatin is dissolved. Cool slightly and stir in the lemon juice. Using an electric mixer, beat the cream and vanilla until soft peaks form. Beat in the lukewarm gelatin mixture very gradually, and continue to beat until stiff peaks form. Whisk the lemon curd until smooth. Fold into the whipped cream, mixing gently until smooth.

TO ASSEMBLE: Reserve $\frac{1}{4}$ of the lemon mousse. Place the cake layer on a serving plate. Pipe or spread $\frac{1}{2}$ of the remaining lemon mousse over the surface of the cake, making sure the mousse comes just to the edge of the cake. Place one of the meringue layers over the mousse. Pipe or spread the second half of the mousse over the meringue layer. Place the second meringue layer over the mousse. Spoon the reserved mousse into a piping bag with a star tip and pipe 12 large rosettes around the edge of the top layer. Sprinkle with toasted almonds. Store refrigerated in a closed container for up to 3 days.

Carrot Cake

Makes one 10-inch (25-cm) layer cake (serves 12 to 14)

FOR THE CAKE:

4 eggs

1¼ cups (300 mL) granulated sugar

1½ cups (360 mL) oil

½ cup (120 mL) Grand Marnier

1 tsp. (5 mL) vanilla extract

2½ cups (600 mL) all-purpose flour

2 tsp. (10 mL) baking powder

1½ tsp. (7.5 mL) baking soda

1 tsp. (5 mL) salt

1 tsp. (5 mL) ground nutmeg

1 tsp. (5 mL) ground cinnamon

2 cups (475 mL) grated carrots

1 cup (240 mL) crushed pineapple

¾ cup (180 mL) broken walnuts

1 cup (240 mL) sweetened flaked coconut

1 cup (240 mL) raisins (optional)

If there ever was a cake for which everyone claims to have the ultimate, best-in-the-world recipe, it is carrot cake. Be forewarned: do not issue any challenges—it is sensitive territory. As always, the proof of the pudding is in the eating. Bake your masterpiece, make no claims and let your audience be the judge. Once they've tasted this version, I can assure you that you won't have to toot your own horn, you can just sit back and bask in the compliments. I have heard "This is absolutely the very best carrot cake I have ever eaten, and I've tasted a lot of carrot cakes!" enough times to feel brave enough to stand behind this claim. The strange thing is, recipes for carrot cake don't vary much. They are usually quite similar, but it seems there exists the all-important, elusive balance of moisture, spices and stickiness that makes the "Perfect Carrot Cake." I hope this works for you.

FOR THE CAKE: Preheat the oven to 350°F (175°C). Butter three 10-inch (25-cm) cake pans and line the bottoms with parchment paper.

Using an electric mixer, beat the eggs and sugar until pale and creamy. Add the oil, liqueur and vanilla and beat until well combined. Sift the flour, baking powder, baking soda, salt, nutmeg and cinnamon. Add to the egg mixture. Stir in the carrots, pineapple, walnuts, coconut and raisins, if using. Pour the batter evenly into the prepared pans. Bake for 25 to 30 minutes, or until a cake tester inserted in the center of the cake comes out clean.

Cool completely before removing from the pans. Wrap in plastic, without removing the parchment, and refrigerate for 2 hours before assembling. (This step chills the soft frosting sufficiently during assembly so that it doesn't ooze out the sides of the cake.)

FOR THE FROSTING:

1 ½ cups (360 mL) cream
    cheese, softened

½ cup (120 mL) butter,
    softened

5 cups (1.2 L) icing sugar

½ tsp. (2.5 mL) almond
    extract

1 tsp. (5 mL) vanilla extract

1 Tbsp. (15 mL) orange zest

1 Tbsp. (15 mL) lemon juice

1 cup (240 mL) chopped wal-
    nuts or coconut, toasted

FOR THE FROSTING: Using an electric mixer, beat the cream cheese and butter until smooth. Add the icing sugar, almond extract, vanilla and orange zest, and beat until smooth and creamy. Add the lemon juice and continue beating until light and fluffy.

Peel the parchment paper off the cake layers. Place one cake on a serving plate. Spread with about ¾ cup (180 mL) of the frosting and top with a second cake. Spread the second layer with ¾ cup (180 mL) of the frosting and top with the third cake. Spread the top and sides of the cake with the remaining frosting. Decorate either the top or sides with the toasted nuts or coconut. Store refrigerated in a closed container for up to 5 days.

Old-Fashioned Oatmeal Cake

Makes one 9 x 13-inch (23 x 33-cm) cake (serves 12 to 16)

FOR THE CAKE:

1 cup (240 mL) old-fashioned rolled oats (not instant or quick)

1½ cups (360 mL) hot water

1⅓ cups (320 mL) all-purpose flour

1 tsp. (5 mL) baking soda

½ tsp. (2.5 mL) baking powder

½ tsp. (2.5 mL) salt

1 tsp. (5 mL) ground cinnamon

½ tsp. (2.5 mL) ground nutmeg

½ cup (120 mL) butter, softened

1 cup (240 mL) granulated sugar

1 cup (240 mL) brown sugar

2 eggs

1 tsp. (5 mL) vanilla extract

FOR THE FROSTING:

1 cup (240 mL) chopped pecans or walnuts

1 cup (240 mL) flaked coconut

⅔ cup (160 mL) brown sugar

⅓ cup (80 mL) butter, melted

½ cup (120 mL) half-and-half

1 tsp. (5 mL) vanilla extract

I found this recipe scrawled in an old notebook from 1977, and although I haven't actually made it in as long, I decided to include it for sentimental reasons. I'm sure many of you will recognize it as something your mother or grandmother used to prepare. This traditional down-home cake, popular with children and great for picnics or potlucks, is easily thrown together, baked, frosted and served all in one pan. The only liberty I've taken with the recipe is to use half-and-half in place of the original canned evaporated milk.

FOR THE CAKE: Butter and flour a 9 x 13-inch (23 x 33-cm) baking pan. Combine the oats and hot water, and set aside to cool. Preheat the oven to 350°F (175°C).

Combine the flour, baking soda, baking powder, salt, cinnamon and nutmeg. Using an electric mixer, cream the butter and both sugars until light and fluffy, about 3 to 4 minutes. Add the eggs and vanilla and beat until smooth. Add the oat mixture and flour mixture alternately to the creamed mixture, beating until just combined. Spread in the prepared pan. Bake for 45 to 55 minutes, just until a cake tester inserted in the center of the cake comes out clean. Cool in the pan.

FOR THE FROSTING: Stir all the frosting ingredients together. Place the oven rack on the second setting down from the broiler. Heat the broiler. Spread the frosting over the top of the cake. Place the pan under the broiler. Broil for 2 to 3 minutes, until golden and bubbly. Cool. Store covered at room temperature for up to 3 days.

Holiday Specials

For most of us, some of the fondest and most cherished memories we have of the holidays are of unpacking boxes of homemade treats and devouring special, once-a-year desserts. Many luscious, over-the-top goodies are perfectly in keeping with the festive mood of the holiday season, and waiting for them all year makes them even more special.

Sugar Cookies

Makes 2 to 3 dozen cookies

½ cup (120 mL) butter,
softened

¾ cup (180 mL) granulated
sugar

1 egg

1 tsp. (5 mL) vanilla extract

½ tsp. (2.5 mL) almond
extract

1 ¼ cups (300 mL) all-purpose
flour

½ tsp. (2.5 mL) baking
powder

⅛ tsp. (.5 mL) salt

1 recipe Royal Icing
(page 210)

Who has time anymore to mess around decorating fussy sugar cookies with colored icing and sprinkles? Apparently lots of people! I, for one, will gladly miss sleep and stay up half the night making pretty Christmas cookies. It is a most soul-satisfying experience and if you've never taken the time I strongly urge you to give it a go. Gather your friends, your kids, your neighbors and make a party of it. The paste food colorings found in bakery supply stores give deep intense Christmas colors, but why not go completely in the opposite direction and do a whole pastel palette for your Christmas cookies? Use white icing with just a hint of pink, lavender, lime green, peach, yellow or aqua for a pretty, sophisticated and delightfully retro look.

Using an electric mixer on medium speed, beat the butter and sugar until light and fluffy, about 2 minutes. Beat in the egg, vanilla and almond extract. Stir in the flour, baking powder and salt, mixing until just combined. Divide into 4 portions, flatten into disks 1 inch (2.5 cm) thick, wrap in plastic and refrigerate until firm, about 30 to 40 minutes.

Preheat the oven to 325°F (165°C). Line two 12 x 18-inch (30 x 45-cm) baking sheets with parchment paper. On a lightly floured board roll out each disk to about ⅛ inch (.3 cm). Cut out using holiday-shaped cookie cutters. For hanging cookies, pierce ½ inch (1.2 cm) from the top edge with a ⅛-inch (.3-cm) round cutter. Place on the cookie sheets. Bake for 10 to 12 minutes, until the edges are golden. Cool for at least 2 minutes in the pans before removing to a rack to cool completely. If not decorating immediately, store the cookies in a tightly closed container.

Pipe or paint the icing on the cookies. Sprinkle the cookies while still wet with colored sugar or silver sprinkles. Allow to dry completely for 24 hours before storing. Store in a tightly closed container with sheets of waxed paper between each layer for up to 1 week. Thread colored ribbons in the precut holes if the cookies are to be hung.

VARIATION

STAINED GLASS COOKIES: These cookies are ridiculously simple to make, and with their clear, brilliantly colored candy center, they look marvelous hanging on the Christmas tree. After cutting out the cookies and placing them on the parchment paper, cut out the centers with a smaller cookie cutter. Fill the centers with crushed colored hard candies. (Don't skimp on the amount of candy, otherwise the center will be too thin). Bake as for regular cookies, but allow the centers to harden before removing the cookies to a rack to cool.

Thumbprint Cookies

Makes 3 dozen cookies

1 cup (240 mL) butter,
  softened

⅔ cup (160 mL) granulated
  sugar

2 eggs, separated

2 tsp. (10 mL) lemon zest

½ tsp. (2.5 mL) almond
  extract

1 tsp. (5 mL) vanilla extract

2 cups (475 mL) all-purpose
  flour

¼ tsp. (1.2 mL) salt

1½ cups (360 mL) almonds,
  finely chopped

¼ to ⅓ cup (60 to 80 mL)
  raspberry jam

I have been making this cookie for as long as I can remember; it is one of my sentimental favorites. Also called a thimble cookie, it gets its name from the indention in the center where the jam is spooned after baking. So get out your thimbles and see how simple it is to create these crumbly, buttery mouthfuls. (What do you mean, you don't have a thimble? Oh, all right, I guess your thumbs will do!)

Preheat the oven to 325°F (165°C). Line two 12 x 18-inch (30 x 45-inch) baking sheets with parchment paper.

Using an electric mixer on medium speed, or a wooden spoon, cream the butter and sugar until light and fluffy. Add the egg yolks, lemon zest, almond extract and vanilla, and beat until combined. Add the flour and salt to the butter mixture and mix until smooth. Using a 1¼-inch (3-cm) ice cream scoop or a teaspoon, form the dough into balls. (Chill the dough for 20 minutes if it seems too sticky to roll.) Use a fork or a small whisk to beat the egg whites slightly. Roll the cookie balls in the beaten egg whites and then in the chopped almonds. Place on the prepared cookie sheets about 2 inches (5 cm) apart. Using your thumb (or a thimble if you have one) make an indentation in the center of each cookie, about ¾ of the way down into the cookie. Wiggle it a bit to spread the opening, especially at the top.

Bake for 15 to 20 minutes, until golden. Cool for about 10 minutes and then fill the indention of the cookies with jam. When completely cool, store in single layers in a tightly closed container for up to 1 week. If keeping more than a week, freeze cookies before adding the jam.

Visions of Sugarplums

Makes 5 to 6 dozen cookies

¼ cup (60 mL) honey

1 tsp. (5 mL) ground
cinnamon

½ tsp. (2.5 mL) ground
allspice

½ tsp. (2.5 mL) ground
nutmeg

3 tsp. (15 mL) orange zest

1 Tbsp. (15 mL) orange juice

1 Tbsp. (15 mL) brandy

2 cups (475 mL) toasted
almonds, finely chopped

¾ cup (180 mL) dried apricots, finely chopped

¾ cup (180 mL) dates, finely
chopped

½ cup (120 mL) dried figs,
finely chopped

¾ cup (180 mL) icing sugar

Is there really such a thing as a sugarplum? I searched everywhere for recipes, but finding them proved somewhat elusive and the ones that I did find varied somewhat. They all contained dried fruit, nuts, spices and, of course, sugar, but lo and behold—no plums! You certainly could include dried plums (or prunes, as they are known), but the name "sugarplum" is more about how they look than what is in them. I urge you to try this recipe even if you are not a fan of dried fruit. These little morsels truly do live up to the magical image their name invokes.

Combine the honey, cinnamon, allspice, nutmeg, orange zest, orange juice and brandy. Add the almonds, apricots, dates and figs and mix thoroughly. Scoop the mixture into ¾-inch (2-cm) balls and roll in icing sugar. Allow to ripen for at least 3 days by placing them in a single layer in a tightly closed container. Store in a single layer in a tightly closed container for up to 3 weeks.

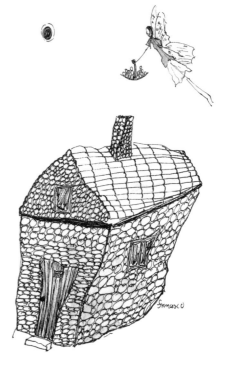

Spice Nut Cookies

Makes 3 dozen cookies

½ cup (120 mL) butter,
softened

½ cup (120 mL) granulated
sugar

½ cup (120 mL) brown sugar

1 egg

1 tsp. (5 mL) vanilla extract

⅔ cup (160 mL) finely ground
pecans or walnuts

1¼ cups (300 mL) all-purpose
flour

1½ tsp. (7.5 mL) baking
powder

¼ tsp. (1.2 mL) salt

½ tsp. (2.5 mL) ground
cinnamon

½ tsp. (2.5 mL) ground
nutmeg

¼ tsp. (1.2 mL) ground cloves

2 egg whites

1 tsp. (5 mL) water

granulated sugar and ground
cinnamon for sprinkling

1 recipe Royal Icing
(page 210) (optional)

With apologies to all you gingerbread lovers, I confess that I tolerate gingerbread only as a building material. It is perfect for making delightfully decorative dwellings or sturdy Christmas tree ornaments, which thankfully do not require being eaten to fulfill their destiny. These little gems, although containing neither molasses nor ginger, have a spicy flavor similar to gingerbread. However, they could never be mistaken for their cardboard cousins. They are tender, buttery rich, fragrant with spices and glazed with a crispy sugar coating—perfect for decorating or just for nibbling. (Don't worry, you gingerbread fanatics, gingerbread cookies are on the next page.)

Using an electric mixer on medium speed, beat the butter and both sugars until light and fluffy, about 2 minutes. Beat in the egg and vanilla until just combined. Combine the nuts, flour, baking powder, salt, cinnamon, nutmeg and cloves, and add to the butter mixture. Stir until just combined. Divide the dough in quarters and flatten each piece into a 1-inch-thick (2.5-cm) disk. Wrap in plastic and refrigerate until firm, about 30 to 40 minutes.

Preheat the oven to 325°F (165°C). Line two 12 x 18-inch (30 x 45-cm) baking sheets with parchment paper. On a lightly floured surface, roll out each disk to about ⅛ inch (.3 cm), and cut into holiday shapes. Whisk the egg whites and water together and brush over the cookies. Sprinkle with sugar and cinnamon. Bake for 10 to 12 minutes, until the edges are golden. Decorate with colored icing if desired. Store in a tightly closed container, layered with sheets of waxed paper. Freeze if keeping for more than 1 week.

Gingerbread Cookies

Makes 4 to 6 dozen, depending on size

1 ¼ cups (300 mL) butter,
   softened

1 cup (240 mL) brown sugar

2 eggs

⅔ cup (160 mL) molasses

4 ½ cups (1.1 L) all-purpose
   flour

1 ½ tsp. (7.5 mL) baking soda

½ tsp. (2.5 mL) salt

½ tsp. (2.5 mL) ground cloves

1 tsp. (5 mL) ground ginger

½ tsp. (2.5 mL) ground
   cinnamon

½ tsp. (2.5 mL) ground
   nutmeg

1 recipe Royal Icing
   (page 210)

My husband, David, who loves anything made with molasses and has even been seen eating the sticky stuff straight out of the can, threatened to quit his job as an official tester of recipes for this book if I didn't include gingerbread cookies. So, although I'm not personally a great fan of this cookie, I concede that it is now time to extol the many virtues of gingerbread cookies and give them their due. They are certainly the perfect cookies to cut into Christmas shapes and decorate; they are easy to roll, sturdy, keep their shape after baking, and have a wonderful molasses ginger flavor that does not fade even after hanging on the tree for days. The dubious palatability of most gingerbread cookies is largely due to the absence, or, at best, stinginess of butter in the recipe—they are built for strength not tenderness. Of course, if you're building gingerbread houses or even more involved structures, like the CN Tower or Taj Mahal, strength and stability are of the utmost importance and a more durable, less tender dough is desirable. But if these cookies are destined to be devoured, by all means load on the butter; they should be tender and delicious as well as beautiful.

Using an electric mixer and a large bowl, beat the butter and brown sugar until smooth. Add the eggs and molasses and beat until fluffy. Combine the remaining ingredients (except the Royal Icing) in a separate bowl. Add to the molasses mixture and beat until combined. Divide into 4 disks, wrap in plastic and refrigerate for a minimum of 2 hours.

Preheat the oven to 325°F (165°C). Line two 12 x 18-inch (30 x 45-cm) baking sheets with parchment paper. Roll out the dough on a lightly floured board to a thickness of ⅛ inch (.3 cm). Cut into shapes, using Christmas cookie cutters. For hanging cookies, pierce ½ inch (1.2 cm) from the top edge with a ⅛-inch (.3-cm) round cutter.

Transfer to the cookie sheets. Bake for 12 to 15 minutes, until firm. Cool on a rack. Decorate the cookies with Royal Icing

Shortbread Cookies

Makes 3 to 4 dozen cookies, depending on size and thickness

1 cup (240 mL) cold butter, cut into ¼-inch (.6-cm) pieces

¼ cup (60 mL) icing sugar

2 Tbsp. (30 mL) fine sugar

¼ cup (60 mL) brown sugar

1⅔ cups (400 mL) all-purpose flour

⅓ cup (80 mL) cornstarch or rice flour

¼ tsp. (1.2 mL) salt

1 tsp. (5 mL) vanilla extract

1 tsp. (5 mL) almond extract

These tender, crispy, melt-in-your mouth morsels are so easy to make and even easier to eat. Shortbread cookies are the simplest thing in the world, and yet the recipes for this traditional treat are many and varied. Usually the differences are slight, both in the ingredients and the technique. I have found, after much experimenting, that I prefer the texture of shortbread when the dough is made with cold butter and is not creamed or overmixed. I also like the tender melting texture that cornstarch or rice flour give to the finished cookie.

Preheat the oven to 400°F (200°C). Line two 12 x 18-inch (30 x 45-cm) baking sheets with parchment paper.

Using an electric mixer with the paddle attachment, or a wooden spoon, beat all the ingredients until the mixture is crumbly and moist but not yet sticky.

Turn the mixture out onto a clean work surface. Divide the dough into 4 equal parts and press each part into a 4-inch-long (9-cm) cylinder. For smaller cookies make a 6-inch-long (15-cm) cylinder. Flatten the ends neatly. Wrap in plastic and chill until firm, about 40 minutes.

Cut each cylinder into 8 to 12 equal slices, depending on the desired thickness of the cookies. Place 1½ inches (3.8 cm) apart on the prepared baking sheets. Reduce the oven temperature to 300°F (150°C) Bake for 20 to 25 minutes, until the edges are pale golden. Cool for 2 minutes before removing to a rack to cool completely. Store in a tightly closed container with sheets of waxed paper between each layer. Freeze if keeping for more than 1 week.

NOTE: If preferred, this dough can also be rolled and cut into various Christmas shapes. Mix for a few seconds longer, until it forms a smooth dough, and then press it into disks rather than cylinders. Chill until firm but allow it to soften slightly before rolling. Bake as above.

Strawberry Mocha Meringue Torte,
page 178

Fresh Peach Melba Cheesecake,
page 158

Mango Chiffon Cheesecake,
page 150

Shortbread Cookies, page 192;
Hazelnut Chocolate Shortbread
Cookies, page 193

Hazelnut Chocolate Shortbread Cookies

Makes 3 to 4 dozen cookies

1 cup (240 mL) cold butter,
  cut into ¼-inch (.6-cm)
  pieces
1⅔ cups (400 mL) all-purpose
  flour
⅓ cup (80 mL) cornstarch or
  rice flour
¼ cup (60 mL) icing sugar
½ cup (120 mL) brown sugar
1 tsp. (5 mL) vanilla extract
¼ tsp. (1.2 mL) salt
2½ cups (600 mL) toasted
  hazelnuts, very finely
  chopped
6 oz. (180 g) semisweet
  chocolate, coarsely chopped
1 cup (240 mL) toasted hazelnuts, finely chopped
3 to 4 dozen whole toasted
  hazelnuts

Irresistible mouthfuls, these flavorful morsels showcase chocolate and toasted hazelnuts—a delicate and sophisticated combination. Perfect any time.

Using an electric mixer with a paddle attachment, or a wooden spoon, beat the butter, flour, cornstarch or rice flour, sugars, vanilla, salt and the 2½ cups (600 mL) very finely chopped nuts until the mixture is crumbly and moist but not yet sticky.

Turn the mixture out onto a clean work surface. Divide the crumbly dough into 4 equal parts and press each part into a 4-inch-long (9 cm) cylinder. For smaller cookies make a 6-inch (15-cm) cylinder. Flatten the ends neatly. Wrap in plastic and chill until firm, about 40 minutes. Preheat the oven to 400°F (200°C). Line two 12 x 18-inch (30 x 45-cm) baking sheets with parchment paper.

Cut each cylinder into 8 to 12 equal slices, depending on the desired thickness of the cookies. Place 1½ inches (3.8 cm) apart on the prepared cookie sheets. Reduce the oven temperature to 300°F (150°C). Bake for 20 to 25 minutes, until the edges are golden brown. Cool.

Melt the chocolate in a double boiler over hot water or in a microwave, stirring occasionally. Dip each cookie halfway into the chocolate and then into the 1 cup (240 mL) chopped nuts. Place on parchment paper and decorate with a whole hazelnut dipped halfway in chocolate. Pack in a tightly closed container, with sheets of waxed paper between layers. Freeze if keeping more than 1 week.

Magic Mountains

Makes 3 to 4 dozen pieces

FOR THE BASE:

1 cup (240 mL) icing sugar

½ cup (120 mL) sliced blanched almonds

2 egg whites, room temperature

2 ½ Tbsp. (37.5 mL) granulated sugar

½ tsp. (2.5 mL) almond extract

FOR THE GANACHE:

1 ¾ cups (420 mL) whipping cream

8 oz. (225 g) semisweet chocolate, coarsely chopped

1 Tbsp. (15 mL) Grand Marnier

Possibly you've had the pleasure of meeting these little treats under a different name—as Sarah Bernhardts, named after the legendary actress. The first time I tasted these velvety smooth morsels, I rushed home and immediately tried to duplicate them. The first attempt produced rather clumsy—albeit delicious—little hills that we promptly called "magic mountains." Inelegant as the name was, it stuck, even though my subsequent creations were much prettier. Call them what you wish, they are sublime and definitely worth the somewhat involved preparation.

FOR THE BASE: Preheat the oven to 325°F (165°C). Line a 12 x 18-inch (30 x 45-cm) baking sheet with parchment paper.

Using a food processor, grind the icing sugar and almonds for 2 to 3 minutes, until finely ground. Scrape the bowl occasionally to loosen the mixture. Continue processing until very finely ground, 2 to 3 minutes more. Sift into a medium bowl.

Using an electric mixer, beat the egg whites until soft peaks form, about 2 minutes. Add the granulated sugar gradually, beating until soft but glossy. Beat in the almond extract. Fold in the sifted almond mixture gently. Using a pastry bag with a plain tip, pipe 1-inch (2.5-cm) rounds about 1 inch (2.5 cm) apart on the prepared pan. Let stand for 20 minutes. Bake the cookies for about 15 to 20 minutes, or until they begin to color. Cool on the pan, and then carefully peel the cookies from the parchment paper. Store in a tightly closed container.

FOR THE GANACHE: Heat the cream to boiling over low heat. Pour over the chocolate in a medium metal bowl. Stir briefly and let sit for 15 minutes, then stir until smooth. Stir in the liqueur. Cover and refrigerate until very cold, at least 3 hours. Stir occasionally to ensure even, rapid chilling.

Using an electric mixer, beat the chilled ganache briefly, just until it begins to stiffen. Be careful not to overbeat, or the ganache will become grainy. Using a pastry bag with a wide tip,

FOR THE GLAZE:

8 oz. (225 g) semisweet
chocolate, coarsely chopped

¾ cup (180 mL) butter

1 Tbsp. (15 mL) corn syrup

2 oz. (57 g) milk chocolate,
finely chopped (optional)

pipe 2-inch (5-cm) conical mounds on top of each cookie base. Refrigerate until firm.

FOR THE GLAZE: Combine the semisweet chocolate, butter and corn syrup in a medium bowl. Place over a pot of simmering water and stir until melted. Remove from the heat and cool to lukewarm. Holding the cookies upside down, dip them in the cooled glaze, covering the ganache completely with the chocolate. Refrigerate until set. Decorate with drizzles of melted milk chocolate, if desired. Store refrigerated in a closed container for up to 4 days.

Cherry Almond Fudge

Makes 3 to 4 dozen pieces

I: THE CLASSIC

1 cup (240 mL) dried cherries

3 Tbsp. (45 mL) amaretto or
   cherry brandy

2 cups (475 mL) granulated
   sugar

1 cup (240 mL) whipping
   cream

½ cup (120 mL) milk

⅓ cup (80 mL) corn syrup

⅓ cup (80 mL) cocoa

2 oz. (57 g) unsweetened
   chocolate, finely chopped

3 cup (60 mL) butter

1 tsp. (5 mL) vanilla extract

1 cup (240 mL) slivered
   almonds, toasted

Here I go again with cherries and chocolate; I just can't help myself! Neither will you once you get a taste of this amazing stuff. I have included two versions of this recipe. The first is a somewhat more time-consuming, authentic rendition of chocolate fudge. The second recipe takes hardly any time at all to prepare and I confess I make it more often for that very reason. Although it certainly is a treat well worth waiting for, instant gratification greatly enhances the overall experience. I highly recommend beginning with the quickie version, preferably a double batch just to get acquainted. Later, when you've had the inevitable one piece too many, you can make plans for trying the long version.

THE CLASSIC: Butter a 9 x 9-inch (23 x 23-cm) pan. Combine the cherries and liqueur in a small bowl. Soak, stirring occasionally.

Combine the sugar, cream, milk, syrup, cocoa and chocolate in a heavy saucepan. Cook over medium heat, stirring until the sugar dissolves and the mixture just begins to boil. Stop stirring and cook over medium heat until it reaches the soft-ball stage, 235° to 240°F (112° to 115°C). (When dropped in ice water it will form a soft but solid ball.) Remove from the heat and add the butter and vanilla. Do not stir. Let cool to about 150°F (65°C). Beat with a wooden spoon until the mixture thickens and loses its sheen.

Drain the cherries. Stir the cherries and almonds into the fudge and spread in the prepared pan. Allow to set for a few hours before cutting into small pieces. Store in a tightly closed container with waxed paper between the layers for up to 2 weeks.

II: THE QUICKIE

1 cup (240 mL) dried sour cherries

3 Tbsp. (45 mL) amaretto or cherry brandy

14 oz. (397 g) bittersweet or semisweet chocolate, coarsely chopped

14-oz. (398-mL) can sweetened condensed milk (1 ⅔ cups/400 mL)

¼ cup (60 mL) butter

1 tsp. (5 mL) vanilla

1 cup (240 mL) sliced almonds, toasted

THE QUICKIE: Line a 9 x 9-inch (23 x 23-cm) pan with two 9 x 14-inch (23 x 36-cm) pieces of parchment paper, overlapping them in the center. Combine the cherries and liqueur in a small bowl. Soak for 30 minutes, stirring occasionally.

In a medium saucepan over low heat or in the microwave, melt the chocolate with the condensed milk, stirring until smooth. Drain the cherries. Stir in the butter until melted, then add the vanilla, drained cherries and almonds. Stir until combined. Spread evenly in the prepared pan and refrigerate for 2 hours.

Remove the slab by lifting up the ends of the parchment paper. Cut into small pieces and store in a tightly closed container with waxed paper between the layers for up to 2 weeks.

Vanilla Fudge

Makes 4 dozen pieces

1 cup (240 mL) whipping
   cream
½ cup (120 mL) milk
3 cups (720 mL) granulated
   sugar
1 cup (240 mL) corn syrup
¼ cup (60 mL) butter
2 tsp. (10 mL) vanilla extract
2 cups (475 mL) toasted
   almonds

My first foray into the kitchen as a young girl was to make fudge. One Christmas when I was 8 or 9 years old, I received a baking kit, complete with miniature rolling pin, cookie cutters and tiny recipe booklet. I was hooked, particularly on the maple fudge. If you've never made fudge before or it's been years since you have, try this recipe. You'll agree that Christmas is the perfect season to whip some up for serving to your guests, for packaging in festive ribbons as gifts, or just for nibbling at home with the family.

Butter a 9 x 9-inch (23 x 23-cm) baking pan. Combine the cream, milk, sugar and corn syrup in a heavy saucepan over medium heat. Stir until the mixture comes to a boil. Stop stirring and continue to cook over medium heat until the mixture reaches the soft-ball stage, 235°F to 240°F (112°C to 115°C). (A small amount dropped in ice water will form a soft but solid ball.) Remove from the heat and allow to cool without stirring to about 150°F (65°C); it will take about 20 to 30 minutes. Beat with a wooden spoon until the mixture thickens and loses its sheen. Add the nuts and spread in the prepared pan. Allow to set for a few hours before cutting. Store in a tightly closed container with waxed paper between the layers for up to 2 weeks.

VARIATION

MAPLE WALNUT FUDGE: Substitute light brown sugar for the white sugar and fresh walnuts for the toasted almonds. Add 1 tsp. (5 mL) maple extract if available, but it really is not necessary, as the combination of brown sugar and walnuts is surprisingly reminiscent of maple.

English Toffee Crunch

Makes about 3 dozen pieces

1 cup (240 mL) butter

1¼ cups (300 mL) granulated
sugar

2 Tbsp. (30 mL) corn syrup

3 Tbsp. (45 mL) water

8 oz. (225 g) semisweet
chocolate, finely chopped

1½ cups (360 mL) pecans or
toasted almonds, finely
chopped

Most of us are familiar with this chocolate-coated candy, having received it as a gift or purchased it in a chocolate shop. The only thing I don't like about this confection is that there is never enough of it. The perfect solution to this problem is to make it yourself. The recipe is quite simple as long as you watch the mixture carefully as it cooks and remove it from the heat at the right moment. Granted, that can be tricky—the first few times I made it I was overly cautious and undercooked it slightly. The result was still delicious but lacked that distinctive, shattering crunchiness that makes this candy so irresistible. Once you've mastered the recipe, I guarantee you'll make it often. It makes a wonderful gift, packed in a colorful tin and wrapped in pretty ribbons.

Butter a 12 x 18-inch (30 x 45-cm) metal pan.

Combine the butter, sugar, corn syrup and water in a large, heavy saucepan. Cook over medium heat, stirring constantly with a wooden spoon, until the butter melts and the sugar dissolves. Cover and boil for about 1 minute. Remove the cover, reduce the heat to medium-low and cook without stirring until the mixture reaches 290°F to 300°F (143°C to 150°C). (A small amount dropped in ice water will form threads that are hard and brittle.) It may be helpful to use a candy thermometer, but I often find them to be inaccurate. It is safer to use the ice-water test. Remove the pan from the heat. Pour the mixture into the prepared pan without stirring. Cool completely to room temperature.

Melt the chocolate in a double boiler over hot water or in the microwave. Spread the melted chocolate over the cooled toffee. Sprinkle with the nuts, pressing them lightly into the chocolate. Let stand at room temperature until the chocolate is completely set. Break into pieces. Store in a tightly closed container for up to 1 week.

"Hands-Off!" Popcorn Nut Crunch

Makes about 12 to 14 cups (3 to 3.5 L)

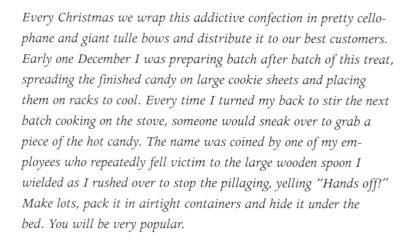

10 cups (2.4 L) popped corn

1¼ cups (300 mL) toasted pecans

1 cup (240 mL) toasted almonds

1⅓ cups (320 mL) granulated sugar

½ cup (120 mL) corn syrup

1 cup (240 mL) butter

1 tsp. (5 mL) vanilla extract

Every Christmas we wrap this addictive confection in pretty cellophane and giant tulle bows and distribute it to our best customers. Early one December I was preparing batch after batch of this treat, spreading the finished candy on large cookie sheets and placing them on racks to cool. Every time I turned my back to stir the next batch cooking on the stove, someone would sneak over to grab a piece of the hot candy. The name was coined by one of my employees who repeatedly fell victim to the large wooden spoon I wielded as I rushed over to stop the pillaging, yelling "Hands off!" Make lots, pack it in airtight containers and hide it under the bed. You will be very popular.

Butter 2 large baking sheets. Combine the popped corn and nuts in a large bowl. Combine the sugar, corn syrup and butter in a very large saucepan. Bring to a boil, stirring occasionally. Cook over medium heat for 10 to 15 minutes, stirring occasionally, until deep golden in color. Add the vanilla carefully; the mixture will sputter. Remove from the heat and stir in the popcorn and nuts. Work quickly to coat the popcorn and nuts completely, as the syrup will harden quickly. Spread the mixture on the prepared baking sheets, breaking it apart into smaller pieces before it hardens completely. Store in a tightly closed container for up to 2 weeks.

Tangerine Crème Brûlée

Serves 6

⅔ cup (160 mL) granulated
  sugar
8 egg yolks
pinch salt
3 cups (720 mL) whipping
  cream
1 entire tangerine peel,
  colored part only, cut into
  very thin strips
1 vanilla bean split lengthwise, or 2 tsp. (10 mL)
  vanilla extract
¼ cup (60 mL) granulated
  sugar

My favorite version of crème brûlée was made with Meyer lemons, but these amazing citrus fruits are grown only for local distribution in California. I confess I smuggled some Meyer lemons back to Canada, buried in my suitcase, risking life and liberty in my pursuit of the perfect crème brûlée. I believe they are a result of crossing lemons with oranges, but this information does nothing to convey the delicate perfume of this remarkable fruit. If you can get your hands on these babies, by all means use them for this recipe; otherwise tangerines, with their subtle, lively aroma, make for a lovely, albeit different, flavor treat.

Preheat the oven to 325°F (165°C). Whisk the ⅔ cup (160 mL) sugar, egg yolks and salt together in a medium bowl. Combine the cream, tangerine peel and vanilla bean (if using vanilla extract, add it later) in a medium saucepan over low heat. Bring slowly to a boil, remove from the heat and scrape the vanilla seeds back into the cream. Discard the bean or rinse it and use it for flavoring sugar. Remove from the heat and let sit for half an hour to allow the vanilla to steep.

Add the warm cream gradually to the egg mixture, whisking continuously until it's thoroughly combined. Add the vanilla extract (if using), and then pour the mixture through a fine mesh strainer. Pour into 6 ovenproof custard cups and place in a shallow baking pan. Pour very hot water around the cups up to ¾ of the height of the cup. Bake for 25 to 30 minutes, or until the custard has set to a shiny, wobbly texture. Remove from the oven carefully and lift the cups out of the pan. Cool to room temperature and then chill for at least 4 hours.

Preheat the broiler. Sprinkle the ¼ cup (60 mL) sugar very evenly over the custards. Broil 3 to 4 inches (7.5 to 10 cm) below the element, just until the sugar melts and turns golden brown. Use a kitchen butane torch if you have one or, if you are very brave, raid the workshop and use a propane torch. Be careful not to actually burn the sugar. Serve immediately.

Spiced Walnut Pie

Makes one 10-inch (25-cm) pie (serves 8)

1 recipe Single Crust Pastry
(see page 31)

5 eggs

1 cup (240 mL) granulated
sugar

1 2/3 cup (400 mL) corn syrup

1 1/2 tsp. (7.5 mL) ground
nutmeg

1 tsp. (5 mL) ground cinnamon

1/2 tsp. (2.5 mL) ground cloves

1/4 tsp. (1.2 mL) salt

1 tsp. (5 mL) vanilla extract

1/4 cup (60 mL) butter, melted

1 1/2 cups (360 mL) very fresh
walnut pieces

1 cup (240 mL) whipping
cream

1 Tbsp. (15 mL) granulated
sugar

1 tsp. (5 mL) vanilla extract

This is an outstanding pie, similar to pecan, with a sweet syrupy custard and crunchy top layer. That's where the similarity ends; the addition of walnuts, cinnamon, cloves and lots of nutmeg creates a unique taste sensation that's very Christmasy.

Prepare the pastry as directed. Preheat the oven to 350°F (175°C).

Using an electric mixer or a whisk, combine the eggs and the 1 cup (240 mL) sugar. Beat just until combined. Beat in the syrup, nutmeg, cinnamon, cloves, salt and vanilla, mixing until smooth. Stir in the butter. Sprinkle the walnuts over the prepared crust and pour in the filling. Bake for 50 to 60 minutes, or until just set. Cool to room temperature before serving.

Just before serving, whip the cream, 1 Tbsp. (15 mL) sugar and remaining 1 tsp. (5 mL) vanilla until stiff peaks form. Serve alongside the pie. Store covered in the refrigerator for up to 5 days.

Jadzia's Poppy Seed Cake

Makes one 10-inch (25-cm) cake (serves 12)

FOR THE CAKE:

3 eggs

1 ¼ cups (300 mL) granulated
  sugar

1 ¼ cups (300 mL) vegetable oil

1 tsp. (5 mL) vanilla extract

2 tsp. (10 mL) lemon zest

2 cups (475 mL) poppy seeds

2 cups (475 mL) all-purpose
  flour

2 tsp. (10 mL) baking powder

¼ tsp. (1.2 mL) salt

1 cup (240 mL) milk

FOR THE GLAZE:

2 Tbsp. (30 mL) water

1 Tbsp. (15 mL) butter

3 Tbsp. (45 mL) granulated
  sugar

3 Tbsp. (45 mL) cocoa

½ tsp. (2.5 mL) vanilla
  extract

I first tasted this wonderfully moist cake, jam-packed with poppy seeds and fragrant with lemon zest, one Christmas many years ago when it arrived at my mother's house with a dear friend of the family, Jadzia Shopian. She gladly provided the recipe after my husband, David, polished off most of the cake. It is easy to prepare, keeps extremely well, and as Jadzia's recipe simply states: "It is a very good cake."

FOR THE CAKE: Preheat the oven to 350°F (175°C). Butter and flour a 10-inch (25-cm) springform pan.

Using an electric mixer, beat the eggs and sugar in a medium bowl until the mixture is pale and thick, about 4 minutes. Add the oil, vanilla and lemon zest; beat thoroughly. Add the poppy seeds and stir until combined. Mix the flour, baking powder and salt together. Add to the poppy seed mixture, alternating with the milk. Combine thoroughly but do not beat. Pour the batter into the prepared pan. Bake for 35 minutes. It should be almost set in the center.

FOR THE GLAZE: While the cake is baking, combine the water, butter, sugar and cocoa in a small saucepan over low heat. Cook, stirring constantly, until the sugar melts and the mixture is smooth. Remove from the heat and stir in the vanilla. Pour over the almost-baked cake and quickly return it to the oven for 10 minutes. Cool completely in the pan before placing on a serving plate. Store covered at room temperature for up to 3 days.

Mincemeatless Pie

Filling for three 10-inch (25-cm) pies

1 recipe Double Crust Pastry
   (page 32; triple the recipe if
   making 3 pies)
½ cup (120 mL) butter, cut
   into ½-inch (1.2-cm) pieces
2 cups (475 mL) brown sugar
¾ cup (180 mL) water
1 tsp. (5 mL) ground cinnamon
1 tsp. (5 mL) ground nutmeg
1 tsp. (5 mL) ground cloves
½ tsp. (2.5 mL) salt
3 cups (720 mL) raisins
1½ cups (360 mL) currants
1½ cups (360 mL) mixed peel
4 cups (950 mL) chopped
   apples
1 cup (240 mL) chopped
   walnuts
2 Tbsp. (30 mL) lemon juice
1 Tbsp. (15 mL) lemon zest
1 cup (240 mL) sour cherries
   (optional)
½ cup (120 mL) brandy
   (optional)
2 egg yolks mixed with
   2 Tbsp. (30 mL) water
sugar, for sprinkling

I know many of you are really not fond of mincemeat, but I urge you to give it a second chance. Made fresh at home without the charming addition of beef snout, ox heart and other unmentionable cow parts found in the original recipe (my apologies to the British), this pie can be absolutely delicious! I especially love baking small tarts that can be eaten in three bites; the extra pastry perfectly balances the sweet richness of the filling. The flavor of the filling benefits greatly from a longer period of cooking. A single batch of filling cooks too quickly, so I've tripled the amount to allow for a longer cooking time. If not used immediately, the filling can be stored in a tightly closed container in the refrigerator for up to one month.

In a large pot, combine the butter, sugar, water, spices and salt. Cook over medium heat until the sugar and spices dissolve. Add the raisins, currants, peel and apples. Continue to cook over medium-low heat, stirring occasionally, until the apples are softened and the mixture is no longer watery, about 1 hour. Add the walnuts, lemon juice, zest, cherries and brandy (if using) and cook for another 15 minutes, stirring occasionally. Store in a covered container in the refrigerator if not using immediately. The flavor improves after 2 or 3 days' storage.

Preheat the oven to 375°F (190°C). Prepare the pastry as directed, setting aside the smaller disk. To make one pie, fill the crust with ⅓ of the filling. On a lightly floured board roll out the smaller disk into a circle ⅛ inch (.3 cm) thick. Using a decorative crimper or knife, cut into four 2-inch (5-cm) strips and five leaves. Using a pastry tip or other small cutter, cut twelve ¼-inch (.6-cm) circles. Make a square lattice of the 4 strips, placing them about 1 inch (2.5 cm) in from the outside edge of the pie. In the center of the square, arrange the five leaves to resemble a poinsettia, attaching the tips of the leaves to the lattice. Fill the center with the circles of pastry. Trim the strips and seal and flute the edges. Glaze with the egg wash. Sprinkle with sugar. Bake for 35 to 45 minutes, until the crust is golden.

The mixture does not need to bubble in the center as it is already cooked. Store lightly covered at room temperature for up to 3 days.

VARIATION

MINCEMEATLESS TARTS: Roll out the pastry as above and cut to fit 2 dozen 2½-inch (6.2-cm) tart pans. Fill and decorate with a pastry star or other Christmas cutout. Brush with egg wash and sprinkle with sugar. Bake until the pastry is golden brown, about 30 minutes.

Extras

What distinguishes a merely so-so dessert from one that is truly spectacular is often something as simple as how it is presented. A fresh berry coulis or a silky custard sauce can add elegant visual appeal as well as contrasting flavors and textures to an otherwise ordinary dessert. A homemade chocolate or caramel sauce can be pulled out of the refrigerator and warmed up in minutes, transforming plain ice cream into a party. Add a few strawberries and you've got a celebration.

Praline

⅔ cup (160 mL) granulated
sugar

⅛ tsp. (.5 mL) cream of tartar

⅓ cup (80 mL) water

1 cup (240 mL) lightly toasted
nuts (hazelnuts, almonds or
pecans), coarsely chopped

This simple crunchy concoction can be used to dress up a variety of tortes and cakes. Ground up and added to mousses or buttercreams, it gives an intense flavor and great texture.

Line a baking sheet with parchment paper. Combine the sugar, cream of tartar and water in a medium saucepan. Cook over low heat until the mixture just begins to boil, stirring occasionally. Continue cooking, without stirring, until the syrup turns pale golden. Add the chopped nuts, swirling the pan to coat the nuts. Continue cooking until the mixture is dark golden brown, about 6 to 8 minutes. Be careful not to let it get too dark. Remove from the heat and spread the nuts onto the parchment paper as thinly as possible. When cool, break the praline into small pieces. Store refrigerated in a covered container for up to 7 days.

Candied Orange Peels

Makes 6 dozen strips

3 or 4 navel oranges

1 ½ cups (360 mL) granulated sugar

⅔ cup (160 mL) water (more as needed)

granulated sugar, for coating

semisweet chocolate, melted (optional)

You'll be amazed at how truly delicious these are when made fresh. An ideal accompaniment to other desserts, they are perfect for nibbling, especially when dipped in chocolate, and make a very welcome gift.

Trim the bottom and top of each orange. Run a knife down the sides of the orange in quarters, cutting through the pith, just to the flesh. Peel off the rind in quarters and slice each into strips ¼ to ⅓ inch (.6 to .8 cm) wide. Cover with water and refrigerate overnight.

Drain and cover with fresh water in a medium saucepan. Bring to a boil over medium heat and cook for about 1 minute. Drain. Combine the sugar with the ⅔ cup (160 mL) water and boil for 1 to 2 minutes. Add the orange strips to the syrup and simmer over low heat for about 50 to 60 minutes, until soft and syrupy, adding water as needed to prevent scorching. Do not stir, but swirl the pan occasionally. Drain. Roll the strips in sugar. Dip in melted chocolate, if desired. Store in a tightly closed container to maintain the soft texture for up to 3 weeks.

NOTE: It is essential to use thick-skinned oranges and to soak the peel overnight to remove the natural bitterness. Do not stir the mixture while it is cooking to prevent crystallization of the syrup.

Royal Icing

Makes 1 cup (240 mL)

2 ½ cups (600 mL) icing sugar
2 egg whites
½ tsp. (2.5 mL) vanilla
  extract
½ tsp. (2.5 mL) almond
  extract

Combine all the ingredients in a medium bowl. Beat with a wooden spoon until smooth. Divide the icing into separate bowls for each color desired. Store icing refrigerated in closed plastic containers. Bring to room temperature before using. Using a piping bag or paper cone, pipe the icing decoratively on the cookies, or paint it on with a brush. You may need to add more icing sugar if the icing is too thin to pipe (it should not spread when applied), or more egg white if the icing is too thick to paint (it should spread smoothly without being transparent).

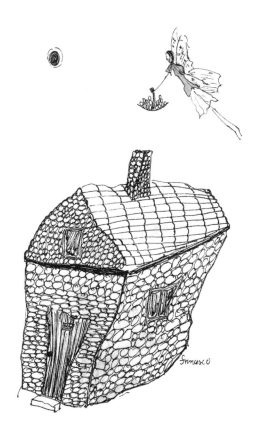

Butterscotch, Fudge and Caramel Sauces

Makes 2 cups (475 mL)

BUTTERSCOTCH SAUCE

2 cups (475 mL) dark brown
    sugar
1 cup (240 mL) corn syrup
½ cup (120 mL) butter
¼ cup (60 mL) water
1 tsp. (5 mL) vanilla extract
1 cup (240 mL) whipping
    cream

FUDGE SAUCE I

1 cup (240 mL) whipping
    cream
½ cup (120 mL) granulated
    sugar
8 oz. (225 g) semisweet
    chocolate, coarsely chopped

FUDGE SAUCE II

1 cup (240 mL) milk
⅓ cup (80 mL) cocoa
⅓ cup (80 mL) corn syrup
1 cup (240 mL) granulated
    sugar
½ cup (120 mL) butter
pinch salt
5 oz. (140 g) semisweet
    chocolate, chopped
1 tsp. (5 mL) vanilla extract

These fast, simple and versatile sauces are perfect on ice cream or as an accompaniment for a multitude of desserts. They are a welcome addition to any cook's repertoire.

BUTTERSCOTCH SAUCE: Combine the sugar, syrup, butter and water in a heavy saucepan. Bring to a boil over medium-low heat, stirring constantly. Cover for 2 minutes and then cook uncovered, without stirring, for 5 minutes. Remove from the heat. Cool for 5 minutes. Stir in the vanilla and whipping cream. Cover and refrigerate for up to 1 month, if not using immediately.

FUDGE SAUCE I: Combine the cream and sugar in a small saucepan. Heat to boiling and stir to dissolve the sugar. Add the chocolate and stir until smooth. Use warm. Cover and refrigerate for up to 1 month, if not using immediately. Reheat as needed.

FUDGE SAUCE II: Combine the milk, cocoa, syrup, sugar, butter and salt in a heavy saucepan. Cook over medium heat, stirring constantly, until the sugar is dissolved and the mixture begins to boil. Reduce the heat to low and simmer for about 10 to 15 minutes without stirring. Remove from the heat and add the chocolate and vanilla. Do not stir. After 15 minutes, stir until just combined. Use warm. Cover and refrigerate for up to 1 month, if not using immediately. Reheat as needed.

CARAMEL SAUCE

1 cup (240 mL) whipping
  cream

1 ¾ cups (420 mL) granulated
  sugar

2 Tbsp. (30 mL) corn syrup

½ cup (120 mL) water

5 Tbsp. (75 mL) butter, cut
  into ½-inch (1.2-cm) pieces

1 tsp. (5 mL) vanilla extract

pinch salt

1 to 2 Tbsp. (15 to 30 mL)
  brandy (optional)

CARAMEL SAUCE: Scald the cream in a medium saucepan and set aside. Combine the sugar, syrup and water in a heavy saucepan. Cover and bring to a boil. Uncover and cook over medium heat, without stirring, until the syrup turns a medium golden color. Swirl the saucepan occasionally. Remove from the heat and add the hot cream slowly, whisking carefully. The mixture will sputter and bubble. Continue stirring until the caramel is completely dissolved. Return to the heat if necessary to dissolve any hardened bits. Stir in the butter, vanilla, salt and brandy, if desired. Use warm or at room temperature. Cover and refrigerate for up to 1 month, if not using immediately.

Crème Fraîche

Makes 1 cup (240 mL)

1 cup (240 mL) whipping
   cream
1 Tbsp. (15 mL) buttermilk

A refreshing change from whipped cream, sweetened crème fraîche can add a sophisticated touch to many desserts, fruit pies in particular.

Combine the cream and buttermilk in a bowl or jar, cover and leave at room temperature for 24 hours. Chill. Crème fraîche will be slightly thicker than sour cream. Store in the refrigerator for up to 1 week.

Raspberry Coulis

Makes about 1½ cups (360 mL)

2 cups (475 mL) fresh or
frozen raspberries
⅓ cup (80 mL) granulated
sugar
1 Tbsp. (15 mL) raspberry-
flavored liqueur (optional)

Ridiculously simple to prepare, a fresh berry coulis adds so much to a dessert. Try it ladled over a rich tarte au citron, drizzled on ice cream, or simply swirled on a serving plate for visual effect.

Thaw the raspberries, if frozen, and reserve the juices. Using a food processor or blender, purée the raspberries. Strain them through a fine mesh sieve. Add the sugar and the reserved juice (if using frozen berries). Stir to dissolve and then add the liqueur, if desired. Store in the refrigerator for up to 3 days.

VARIATION

BLUEBERRY COULIS: Substitute wild blueberries for raspberries. Increase the sugar to ½ cup (120 mL), add 1 tsp. (5 mL) lemon zest to the food processor or blender, and substitute lemon juice for the liqueur.

Crème Anglaise

2 cups (475 mL) half-and-half

4 egg yolks

⅓ cup (80 mL) granulated
  sugar

2 tsp. (10 mL) vanilla extract

A perfect finishing touch to so many desserts, particularly ones made with fruit, this simple custard sauce is wonderful served warm or cold. I prefer it not too sweet and with the added richness of light cream instead of milk.

Scald the cream in a medium saucepan and set aside. Whisk the egg yolks and sugar in a medium bowl until thick and pale, about 3 minutes. Add the hot cream slowly, whisking until smooth. Return to the pot and cook over simmering water, stirring constantly, for about 10 to 15 minutes, until the custard coats the back of the spoon. Remove from the heat and stir in the vanilla. Pour the mixture through a fine strainer. Cool, stirring occasionally. Cover with plastic wrap and refrigerate for up to 4 days.

VARIATION

RASPBERRY CRÈME ANGLAISE: Prepare as for regular Crème Anglaise, but replace the half-and-half with whipping cream. Pureé 1 ¼ cups (300 mL) raspberries and press through a fine strainer. Add the raspberry purée to the cooled custard. Store as above.

Lemon Curd

Makes 2 cups (475 mL)

6 egg yolks

¾ cup (180 mL) granulated
sugar

⅔ cup (160 mL) fresh lemon
juice

½ cup (120 mL) cold butter,
cut into ½-inch (1.2-cm)
pieces

1 Tbsp. (15 mL) lemon zest

*Lemon curd is a refreshing and versatile addition to any dessert
repertoire. Whether served as a glaze, as a basis for mousse,
or as a filling for prebaked tart shells, a tangy citrus curd is
always welcome.*

Whisk the egg yolks and strain through a fine mesh sieve.
Whisk the egg yolks and sugar together in a medium saucepan.
Stir in the lemon juice and cook over medium-low heat, stirring
constantly with a wooden spoon. Do not allow it to come to a
boil. Cook until the mixture coats the back of the spoon.
Remove from the heat and whisk in the butter and lemon zest.
Transfer to a bowl and cover with plastic wrap or pour into
sealed jars and refrigerate for up to 3 weeks.

VARIATIONS

ORANGE CURD: Decrease the sugar to ⅔ cup (160 mL) and
replace the ⅔ cup (160 mL) lemon juice with ½ cup (120 mL)
orange juice and 3 Tbsp. (45 mL) lemon juice. Substitute
1 Tbsp. (15 mL) orange zest for the lemon zest.

LIME CURD: Decrease the sugar to ⅔ cup (160 mL). Substitute
lime juice for the lemon juice and lime zest for the lemon zest.

Index

About the Author

Wanda Beaver's love of baking began at an early age. She baked her first pie when she was nine, using cherries picked from her family's half-acre fruit-filled paradise. Since that first sour cherry pie, she hasn't looked back.

Born and raised in St. Catharines, Ontario, in the heart of Canada's prime fruit-growing area, she pushed her passion for baking aside in favor of more "serious" career aspirations. During her fourth year at the Ontario College of Art, a freshly baked pie for a friend led to her first commercial account. By graduation, she was delivering so many pies, she put her art career on hold (temporarily, she thought), to open a small bakery.

Fifteen years later, Wanda has 20 employees, two retail locations, and more than enough customers to keep her busy baking pies, cookies, cakes, and other sweets. Determined to demystify pie making, she teaches introduction-to-pastry classes and now offers this cookbook, a collection of her yummiest recipes.